£4·95

Practical

MADEIRA

1993

Hayit Publishing

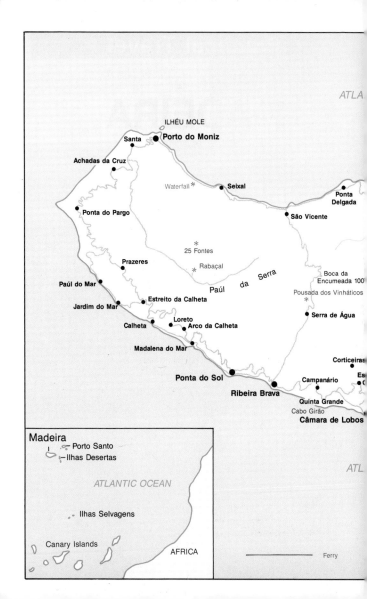

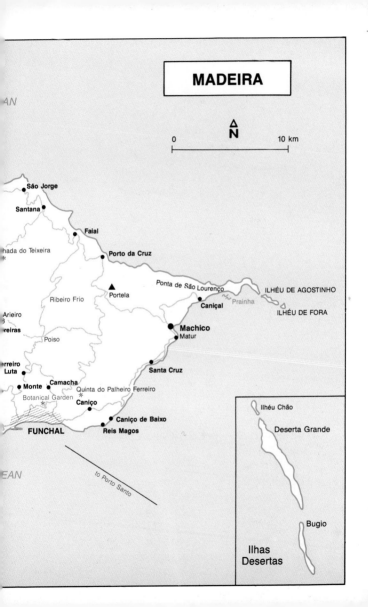

1st Edition 1993
UK Edition: ISBN 1 874251 04 5
US Edition: ISBN 1 56634 014 4

copyright 1993
  UK Edition: Hayit Publishing GB, Ltd, London
  US Edition: Hayit Publishing USA, Inc., New York

copyright 1992 original version: Hayit Verlag GmbH
  Cologne/Germany

Authors: Angelika Trippe, Jutta Steinkötter
Translation: Kathleen Splieth
Adaption, Revision: Scott Reznik
Print: Scholma Druk, Bedum, NL
Photography: Angelika Trippe, Jutta Steinkötter

Using this Book

Books in the *Practical Travel* series offer a wealth of practical information. You will find the most important tips for your travels conveniently arranged in alphabetical order. Cross-references aid in orientation so that even entries which are not covered in depth, for instance "Casa de Abrigo," lead you to the appropriate entry, in this case "Accommodation." Also thematically altered entries are also cross-referenced. For example under the heading "Entering Madeira," there appear the following references: "Travel Documents, Customs Regulations;" under the heading "Driving," the reference "Travel on Madeira."

With travel guides from the *Practical Travel* series the information is already available before you depart on your trip. Thus, you are already familiar with necessary travel documents and maps, even customs regulations. Travel within the country is made easier through comprehensive presentation of public transportation, car rental in addition to the practical tips ranging from medical assistance to newspapers available in the country. Descriptions of cities are arranged alphabetically as well and include the most important facts about the particular city, its history and a summary of significant sights. In addition, these entries include numerous practical tips — from shopping, restaurants and accommodation to important local addresses. Background information does not come up short either. You will find interesting information about the people and their culture as well as the regional geography, history and current political and economic situation.

Contents

Accommodation

Accommodation is mainly concentrated in Funchal's *zona hoteleira* (hotel zone). On the south coast, additional tourist centres have developed in Caniço de Baixo, Reis Magos and near Machico ("Matur").

On the northeast coast there is virtually no accommodation, except in Porto Moniz. In larger towns, such as São Vicente, Ribeira Brava, or Porto Moniz, the number of hotel rooms is being increased in order to bring tourism to these areas as well and thus take some of the pressure off Funchal and the southern coast.

The following briefly describes the various types of accommodation on Madeira. Specific prices and addresses are given under each entry. Tourist information offices can arrange for accommodations free of charge *(→Tourist Information)*.

Guest Houses: As a rule, guest houses are simple, clean, and relatively economical. Double rooms are available from 2500$00, some with a private bath, but usually one bath is shared by several rooms.

Residencial: A residencial is comparable to a middle-class hotel, with double rooms priced from about 4500$00.

Hotels: As already mentioned, most of the hotels are located in the *zona hoteleira* in Funchal. These are of high, international standards. Four five-star hotels provide an exclusive atmosphere. The richest in tradition is the "Reids" hotel — the oldest, most tasteful and stylish of the hotels (incidentally one of the most expensive as well). Its 100-year tradition, 12½-acre tropical garden, 400 employees (about three per guest!), traditional five o'clock tea, and numerous illustrious guests (no less than Winston Churchill, Empress Sissi of Austria, and the King and Queen of Sweden have graced the premises) make for a very special aura, which one notices even passing by. The Scottish founder of this hotel, William Reid, began his own rags-to-riches story in the middle of the 19th century with £5 in his pocket.

Pousada: This is the name given to state-run hotels which are found in historical buildings or amidst especially remarkable scenery. Service and comfort are of a high standard. Reservations are necessary. There are two Pousadas on Madeira *(→Pico do Arieiro, Vinháticos)*.

Casa de Abrigo: Literally translated, this means "house of shelter," but what is meant is a kind of forester's hut. One may spend the night these types of accommodation after making reservations with the regional government in the "Quinta Vigia" in Funchal. Guests must bring their own food. Bedding, dishes, and towels are provided. Accommodation is very basic and are well suited to hikers who want to combine two lengthier tours. One should reserve space as early as possible, since *Casas de Abrigo* are often completely booked months in advance. It is also possible to camp at the huts, but here again one needs a permit obtained at the Office of Agriculture and Forestry in the Rua das Cruzes (Direcção Regional da Agricultura/dos Serviços Forestais) *(→Rabaçal, Pico do Ruivo)*.

Private Rooms: There are almost no private rooms to be had in Funchal. The large selection of professionally-run accommodations and the crowded living conditions of the Madeirans hardly allow for this. In smaller towns, it might be worth asking a taxi driver or in a café about the availability of private rooms.

Holiday Apartments: Holiday apartments for two to five persons are available in the tourist areas of Funchal, Caniço de Baixo, Matur (near Machico), and Reis Magos (→*individual entries*).

→*Camping*

Achada do Teixeira

After having branched off in Santana, road ER 101-5 ends at the Achada do Teixeira. From this point, one can walk to Pico Ruivo in around an hour (→*Pico Ruivo*).

Transportation: Bus no. 103 from Funchal to Santana (toward Boaventura), travel time is around two hours; from Santana by taxi.

Achadas da Cruz

Pristine, mixed laurel forests characterise the landscape around Achadas da Cruz. A livestock market, the *Feira de Gado,* is held in July near Santa. The stands at which livestock is sold are located at the intersection of the ER 204 and the ER 101.

Agriculture

The first settlers would probably not have believed that an island with such dense primeval forests and mostly inaccessible terrain could be so intensively cultivated. The slopes were too steep to be worked, and the soil could only be held through terracing supported by stone walls. The walls are in part built of very heavy basalt blocks and surround small parcels of land with gentler slopes. The fields are still terraced and this landscape — formed through long years of cultivation — is characteristic of the island's lower regions. Nowadays, one can hardly imagine how these hillsides must have looked in their untouched, natural condition. Every little patch of land was and still is used agriculturally; the steeper the slope, the smaller the individual fields. Most fields can only be reached on foot and worked by hand. Both machines and animals are too inefficient under the circumstances to make them economical.

Irrigation was a problem because the south side of the island is relatively dry, and water had to be brought from the north. The Levadas are designed to solve this problem, and are brilliantly constructed to suit the conditions (→*Levadas*).

Approximately fifty percent of the island's area is cultivated, about half used in farming and half in forestry. Crop yields are not sufficient to supply all of the island's needs; thus, many agricultural products are imported from the mainland. The most important agricultural exports to Portugal are bananas and — in limited quantities

— other exotic fruits; wine, flowers, and baskets woven from willow grown on Madeira are exported abroad.

Farms are quite small: 85% of the farmers have less than one hectare of land, composed of many small terraces. Their methods are outdated, the majority of farmers and farm workers belong to the older generation, and many residents farm the land only as a source of supplemental income.

To obtain the most from hard-won arable land, various fodder and vegetable crops are rotated, or the fields are used doubly: vegetables are grown below the grapevines.

Madeira's soil is relatively well suited to farming. The clay-rich, red soil results from the interaction of the native vegetation with the original, loose volcanic rock. On Porto Santo, mostly grain is grown since extensive areas of flat land allow for the use of cattle-drawn plows. Vineyards on Porto Santo produce only enough wine for local consumption. Here, farmers have to cope with the summer drought and combat wind erosion by building walls around their fields.

At the beginning of the 15th century, Dom Henrique "The Seafarer" (→History) introduced *sugar cane* as the first plantation crop. Since then, this has long played an important economic role on the island. The cultivation of sugar cane is limited

Many terraced fields on the mountain slopes are painstakingly tended by hand

to the lower regions on the north and south sides, and today is used only in the manufacture of brandy (Aguardente) and sugar syrup (Mel de Cana). Sugar production reached its height in the 16th century; today, however, it is of little significance.

Wild sugar cane is native to New Guinea. There are also many cultivated varieties since sugar cane has been grown for thousands of years. This is a type of grass, 5 to 8 metres (16 to 26 feet) tall, which requires tropical warmth (18°C or 64°F) and continual irrigation corresponding to conditions in its native environment. The harvest lasts from March to May; the stalks themselves contain up to 20% sugar (→Porto da Cruz).

Banana plantations cover about 8% of the island's area and are mostly concentrated on southern coastal fields under 300 metres (980 feet) in elevation. Nearly 80% of the yield is exported.

According to the type of grape, vineyards are found on the south side at elevations of around 500 metres (1,650 feet), and on the north side between approximately 200 to 300 metres (650 to 980 feet). Harvesting takes place in August (→Wine). Predominantly root crops and other vegetables are grown under the vines.

Common Madeiran crops include *yams, beans, cabbage, carrots, onions, corn* and *taro*. Taro is a swamp plant in the arum family which thrives in moist, warm climates. This tuber has a high starch content and the leaves contain protein, which makes taro a useful fodder crop as well. Likewise, yams produce starch-rich tubers from their root systems. Portions of the plant above the ground can be recognised by the heart shaped leaves and tendril-like runners. Animal husbandry is practised only to a small extent, but in such an unusual way that it is worth mentioning. Cattle are kept in "Palheiros," the small, straw-covered sheds that are scattered evenly across the terraced hillsides. The animals are fed in stalls, so that they need not graze on the precious fields and are not in danger of slipping on the precipitous slopes. Their fodder grows in the bordering fields; thus, fertiliser (dung) is produced directly where it is needed. Most farmers own only one or two head of cattle and a similarly small number of pigs, which are also kept in a limited amount of space. In the mountains and on the high plain Paúl da Serra, sheep and goat herding is the only agricultural use for such inaccessible or inhospitable regions.

Commercial forestry consists primarily of managing pine forests (35,000 acres) and eucalyptus forests (5,000 acres and increasing) for lumber, firewood, and sawdust. Earlier, the laurel forests yielded large quantities of valuable lumber, but today this plant is legally protected (→Flora). Eucalyptus trees have fibrous bark that naturally peels off in strips and sickle-shaped leaves. The scent of these forests is unmistakable. These cultivated plants are, however, not without their drawbacks: they grow rapidly, have fibrous wood that is thus not very valuable, and in monoculture, they quickly dry out the soil.

In addition, acacias and chestnuts (500 hectares each) are grown, the former for lumber and the latter for the edible nuts.

Animals and Wildlife

The Madeiran archipelago is known for its unusual birds and a rich underwater fauna. In contrast, few species of animals were found on land prior to settlement. Today, one encounters countless dogs, some of which are strays. Lizards are equally abundant, and there are nearly a thousand different insect species. Aside from a few mosquitoes and gnats, no larger or dangerous insects are indigenous to the island. Only in the northern half of Deserta Grande does one find the largest species of wolf spider, zoological name *Geolycosa ingens.* This spider is said to be poisonous, but since entry into its area is only rarely allowed, it presents no danger, and even specialists have to search a long while before finding one of these shy creatures. A visit to the natural history museum is less strenuous and safer if one wants to see a prepared specimen of the wolf spider.

Rabbits were brought to the island long ago and, lacking natural predators, they have multiplied astronomically. On Porto Santo, they have periodically reached plague proportions and have become a favourite quarry among hunters, as is also true on Madeira.

The first settlers are said to have lived off of the numerous birds, of which there are a plethora of native as well as migratory species. The dove *Columba trocaz,* for instance, lives in the dense laurel forests and can be found only on Madeira and has meanwhile been placed under protection. Hunting is allowed only during specific times of year. Other doves, partridges and pheasants were also on Madeira's early menu, as were young Cagarras (Madeira gadfly petrel). These sea birds nest in colonies on the Desertas and Selvagens and are also under protection, since they used to be captured by the thousands every year and sold as sweetmeats in the fishing villages.

Several species of seagulls and petrels or other tube-noses are found here as well, including some species which occur only on Madeira and the Canary or Atlantic Islands.

We recommend visiting the natural history museum, whose former director (G. Maul) put together a remarkable collection of the birds of Madeira and the Selvagens.

Aquatic Animals

The underwater fauna is of special interest due to the peculiar conditions created by the island's exposed position and the narrow shelf surrounding the island. Scuba divers and snorkellers will discover parrot fish, sea bass and groupers, mantas, and other shelf inhabitants. Since the closing of many stretches of coast to commercial fishing, fish populations are slowly recovering from the disastrous consequences of overfishing. Illegal fishing with dynamite has had especially catastrophic effects on the fish and seals. The strictest controls possible are necessary to ensure that the fragile shelf ecosystem is not completely destroyed.

Commercial fisheries take advantage of passing schools of tuna, mackerel, and sardines, as well as the ever-present rosefish and dangerous morays. Live bait is used in tuna fishing, which does not decimate the population to the extent that net-fishing can since tuna do not eat when en route to their spawning areas and so ignore the bait. Successful reproduction and replenishment of tuna populations are, therefore, less endangered. Tuna migration is currently being researched; these fish do not always migrate past Madeira. Due to a change in migration patterns, there was no catch in the 1980's, and the tuna factories were forced to close. The main fishing season is February to September; three or four species of tuna are caught.

The black swordfish of the depths, the Espada, is used nowhere as intensively as on Madeira, although it is found in oceans world wide. Japan is the only other country where it is eaten. This slender predatory fish, over three feet in length, is taken from waters 2,500 to 4,000 feet deep with a line of appropriate length, whose end is covered with up to 150 baited hooks. The best fishing hours are during the night, and it is assumed that the fish come up to these "heights" only to seek prey, but otherwise spend their time at even greater depths. Very little is known about their biology since their habitat is not easily accessible for researchers. Such fish are well adapted to the pressure, cold and darkness of these depths, and would die as a result of the tremendous pressure differences before reaching the surface. The Espada is, along with tuna, the most frequently eaten fish throughout the year.

To protect local marine mammals, a 78,000 square mile area surrounding Madeira was set aside in 1985 as a national park — hopefully soon enough to save the monk seals. They were once native to the Mediterranean Sea, but now seem to be nearly extinct worldwide. The population seems to be recovering ever since the southern half of Deserta Grande was placed under complete protection. Even the formerly hunted sperm whale *(→Caniçal/Whale Museum)* and many other species of marine mammals such as finwhales, humpback whales, dolphins and porpoises are given a chance for survival here.

Bargaining

At marketplaces, bargaining with grocers and butchers is hardly appropriate because prices are fixed. However, one can try one's luck at roadside flower or souvenir stands, where it is safe to assume that as a tourist, one will pay a type of "foreigner's tax" in the form of a higher price.

Baskets

Woven baskets have been exported in large quantities only since the end of the 19th century. As was the case with embroidery, it was the English who initiated this export.

The willows, which grow chiefly in the wet river regions in northern Madeira, are cut from January to March. Thin, flexible branches are more valuable than the thicker ones. They are peeled and then boiled in large containers outdoors. Then the willow switches are laid on the roadsides to dry, lending a very picturesque touch to the landscape. Only when dry are they weighed and later sold according to weight. Fabrication takes place mostly in →*Camacha* but many items are still produced domestically. Payment for wicker work is as bad as for embroidery. The main importers are the U.S. and Canada.

Beaches

On Madeira's eastern tip, the Ponta de São Lourenço, there is a tiny sand beach not even 100 yards long. The small bay is fittingly called "Prainha," meaning "little beach," and even this is exaggerated. Some towns and villages lie on bays with pebble or gravel beaches that are hardly suited to swimming and sunbathing.

During the spring, the wicker is laid out to dry

Natural access to the ocean is rare because of the steep, rugged coastline (→*Sports/Swimming*). An excursion to Porto Santo is just the thing when one is in the mood for the beach. Here, one will find a wide beach of fine-grained sand around 7 km (4 miles) long. It is quite full in summer, especially on weekends, but the size of the beach lets the crowd spread out well. During the off-season, one can get a feel for how it was years ago: empty, tranquil, quiet, and thus utterly relaxing. It is at its best in October and November, when the weather is still mild.
→*Porto Santo*

Booksellers

The bookstore "Ypsilon" at Rua da Alfândega 42-46 offers the largest selection of foreign newspapers, magazines, and books, and is open daily from 8 am to 8 pm. At the "Livraria Inglesa," Rua Carreira 43, and at the "Livraria Esperança," Rua dos Ferreiros 119, numerous publications about Madeira are available in English, German, French or Portuguese.

Business Hours

There is no universal official closing time for shops in Portugal. The following represent normal shop and office hours, with possible minor variations:

Fascinating in its dimensions: the four and a half mile long beach of Porto Santo

Banks: Monday to Friday, 8:30 am to 3 pm.

Museums: Hours for museums vary. Inquire locally.

Pharmacies: Monday to Friday from 9 am to 1 pm and 3 to 7 pm; Saturday from 9 am to 1 pm.

Post Office: Monday to Friday from 9 am to 12:30 pm and 2:30 to 5:30 pm (minor variations are possible). The post offices in Funchal have longer hours (→*Funchal/Post Office*).

Shops: Shops have very flexible hours; as a rule of thumb, however, weekdays from 9 am to 1 pm and from 3 to 7 pm. Many "Minimercados" in smaller towns are also open on weekends, because people who live in more remote villages often combine church on Sunday with shopping afterwards, lacking time during the week for a trip into town. In Funchal there are a few supermarkets that are open daily until 9 or even 11 pm.

Cabo Girão

This is the second highest coastal cliff in the world and lies about 18 km (11 miles) west of Funchal and 10 km (6 miles) from Câmara de Lobos. The cliff towers 580 metres (1,897 feet). Coming from Estreito de Câmara de Lobos, just before reaching Cabo Girão, one encounters practically every manifestation of tourism that is inseparable from a world-class attraction: a supermarket and restaurant cleverly called "Cabo Girão," roadside souvenir stands, and parked cars leave no doubt that the cape is near. In front of the restaurant "Cabo Girão," face left toward the coast and "Miradouro," the overlook. From the platform there is a spectacular view all the way to Funchal on one side and Ponta do Sol on the other. Risking a look over the edge, one will be surprised to discover that the minute strip of beach at the bottom is used to grow bananas. Here, one will definitely appreciate what it means to farm on Madeira, when even such inaccessible acres are cultivated. It is said that in the last century, farm workers were lowered down on ropes, and at the end of the day hauled back up again. Nowadays, the farmers reach these fields by boat. The name Cabo Girão is derived from the Portuguese word *giro*, which means "revolution" or "circuit," since it was near here that Zarco ended his first circumnavigation of Madeira.

Transportation: Take bus no. 7 (toward Ribeira Brava), no. 154, or no. 6 (toward Boaventura, operating three times daily).

Calheta

The community of Calheta consists of three main districts, which are worth seeing not only because of the unusual architecture. Beyond Canhas (coming from Funchal) the mountainsides become a world of lush vegetation and at every bend in the road there is yet another beautiful view of the sea. This area is especially intensively farmed; the smallest piece of land is terraced, planted and tended. Local residents make a living from banana plantations, vineyards, and livestock breeding. If travelling by car, one should make a point of stopping at the posted *Miradouros,* or overlooks, to enjoy the scenery.

Arco da Calheta

On the way to Arco da Calheta, there are two *Miradouros,* both of which should not be missed. The first — on the way from Canhas — offers a fantastic view of the ocean.

To find the second *Miradouro,* follow the serpentine road that winds up the mountain. At 846 metres in elevation (2,766 feet), one has only the wooded mountains above, the sea below, and the restaurant "O Farol" to one side.

In Arco da Calheta one can see the chapel *Nossa Senhora do Loreto,* built around 1510. The chapel has been rebuilt many times, and only the south portal remains of the original structure. Should the chapel be closed, one can still get a glimpse through the windows of the impressive blue and white ceiling of Spanish/Moorish origin.

A roof supported by columns was added on to the front of *Nossa Senhora* to accommodate the pious, who flock to this chapel especially for *Romaria* on September 8th *(→Holidays and Celebrations).*

Arco da Calheta is a tiny village whose "centre," comprised of a café and minimercado, is stretched out along the road that has been paved around the ancient, imposing sycamores.

Calheta

During Madeira's golden age, Calheta was an important region for sugar cane production. Even today, sugar cane is cultivated nearby and distilled for *Aguardente,* but in considerably smaller quantities than in bygone eras. An old chimney and steam cooker on Calheta's beach are reminiscent of the sugar cane distillery that once stood here. The factory was founded on November 23, 1909, and in 1989 the buildings and grounds were made into a municipal park. Calheta is a tidy village where domestic gardens are lovingly tended. On the village square, one can relax at the restaurant "Praça Velha." A filling station and another restaurant are located at the edge of town heading toward Estreito da Calheta. No accommodation is available in this village.

Built in the 15th century, the church is Calheta's main attraction. The structure exhibits a Manueline influence, the ceiling is of Spanish/Arabian origin and is, unlike the ceiling in Loreto's Chapel, not embellished with frescoes. Of interest to the art historian are the font, a richly ornamented processional cross, and a sacral shrine, all allegedly a gift from King D. Manuel (1385-1433).

Estreito da Calheta

This little village will tempt those who visit the Church of the Magi, *Dos Reis Magos* to linger. Lovely wood carvings and a three-panel altarpiece depicting the Magi were made in Antwerp in the 16th century. The Spanish/Arabian ceiling and Gothic font are also remarkable.

Transportation: Bus no. 107 (toward Raposeira) operates twice daily from Monday to Friday. The trip lasts around two hours.

Camacha (Madeira)

Camacha is known as the wicker capital of Madeira. Also adding to the town's profile is "Café Relógio," an imposing modern building with a view of the ocean, which combines a wicker factory with exhibitions, a shop, a café, and a restaurant. In the exhibition area — aside from the huge array of baskets, bowls and the like — the furniture on the basement level is especially impressive. Alongside complete sets of wicker furniture, one can also see artfully crafted and unusually large wicker animals. Those who wish to bring home a large piece of furniture as a souvenir, should ask about shipment abroad, which is included in the service. "Café Relógio" is also open on Sundays. (Address: Achada, 9135 Camacha, Tel: 92 21 14/92 24 15). Camacha has a small town square full of greenery, around which village life takes its course. There is a supermarket, the Centro de Saúde, and a bank on the square. This is also where a number of hiking trails begin and end (→Hiking).

Transportation: Buses no. 77 (toward Santo da Serra) and 29 (to Funchal) run almost hourly. The trip lasts about 40 minutes.

Câmara de Lobos

This lively fishing village is about 9 km (5½ miles) west of Funchal along the coast. Its name, which means "seal chamber," comes from the *lobos-marinhos,* the seals which are said to have populated the bay by the hundreds in Zarco's time.

Câmara de Lobos was the first settlement that Zarco founded after Funchal; this in 1420. The explorer himself lived here for several years while the territory around Funchal was being made arable by slash-and-burn clearing. A church was, of course, built in the new settlement, and it is said to be one of the oldest on the island (before 1425).

Zarco was honoured by King D. Afonso V for his role in colonising the island, and was rewarded with (among other things) the epithet "Câmara de Lobos," which was shortened over the years to simply "Câmara," a common surname on the island even today. This little fishing village became well known in the 1950's thanks to England's former Prime Minister, Winston Churchill, who painted village scenes during his holidays here.

Today, a large portion of the population still lives from fishing; bananas and grapevines are grown in the vicinity. As idyllic as Câmara de Lobos might seem at first glance, the living conditions of the villagers are often something else altogether. Many socially disadvantaged individuals with turbulent family backgrounds live in Câmara de Lobos. The begging children that one sees often enough at the wharf in Funchal are mostly from Câmara de Lobos.

On the way from Funchal, one can turn left at the filling station and park the car immediately on the right in front of the market building. From here, the paved street, Rua de Nossa Senhora de Conceição, leads to the wharf. There is a chapel here, too, but the hustle and bustle of the harbour, the fishing boats, and fish drying on rocks or wooden racks are more interesting.

What is special about this place is the natural harbour and densely populated rocky promontories, called *Ilhéu*.

Walking from the fountain up Rua São João de Deus, one comes to probably (it is contested) the oldest church on the island. This richly decorated church with its blue and white tiled tower and baroque decor was renovated in 1723.

The plaza above Rua São João de Deus invites one to linger and enjoy its palm trees, the pavilion and the view of the sea.

Scenic Overlook/Miradouro: There is a very good view of the village from *Pico do Torre,* from which one can observe the harbour and colourful fishing boats, the milling masses at the market in the morning and the pulse of village life. From here, one sees clearly that part of Câmara de Lobos is built on a rise, where the houses are clustered together like mussels on a stone. To reach this point, one must follow the street out of town until reaching a blue and yellow sign which reads

The lively fishing town of Câmara de Lobos even drew Winston Churchill to this area for longer stays

"Miradouro." Continuing up the road and to the right, one comes upon *Pico do Torre* after about one kilometre (½ mile).

Câmara de Lobos/ **Practical Information**

Accommodation: Private apartments can be arranged through "Turismo" only when booked well in advance.

Bank: "Banif" on Rua São João de Deus.

Festival: There is a church consecration festival on June 19 in honour of São Pedro (Saint Peter) patron saint of fishermen.

Transportation: One can easily and quickly reach Câmara do Lobos with any of several westbound busses from Funchal. Numbers 1, 7, 27, and 96 run most frequently. There is one bus stop near the filling station and another across from the market.

Medical Care: There is a sign for the Centro de Saúde on the way into town. It is located on the left-hand side of the street. A doctor can be found at Rua São João de Deus No. 98, and a pharmacy, only a few steps further (No. 46).

Police: The way to the police station is marked, but the police officers speak only Portuguese. Tel.: 94 21 85.

Post Office: From the village plaza with the pavilion, one goes north along the broad street; the post office is on the right-hand side.

Restaurants and Grocers: In the shopping centre on Rua São João de Deus there is a bakery and café next to the supermarket which is highly recommended. For fresh fruit, vegetables, or fish, it is best to shop at the marketplace located in the reddish building.

Naturally, good fish restaurants are part of any fishing village ("Riba Mar," "Coral," "Os Veteranos").

Tourist Information: "Tourismo" is located on the left-hand side of the central plaza with the pavilion and the most restaurants. Private rooms and apartments can be reserved here. Hours: Monday to Friday from 9:30 am to 4:00 pm and Saturday from 9:30 am to 1:00 pm.

Camping

On the entire Madeiran archipelago, there are only two camping areas: on Porto Santo Island and in →*Porto Moniz* on the northwestern coast of Madeira. No additional campgrounds are planned, on the one hand because of the lack of level land, and on the other, due to concern that hoards of so-called backpack-tourists would (as local businesses believe) lower the current intentionally elevated class of tourism. Prices are, however, low in comparison to those elsewhere in Europe, for instance in France.

Both campgrounds are comparatively new and well maintained. During Portuguese summer holidays and on weekends, one must reckon with crowds and a lot of noise and turmoil, at least on Porto Santo since many Madeirans spend their summer holidays there.

The campground in Porto Moniz can only be recommended during the summer being that the northern coast can often be unpleasantly cool and damp in winter and early spring.

Camping in the wilderness or on private property is only allowed with the permission of the landowners and/or local residents. The employees of the *Casas de Abrigo (→Accommodations/Casas de Abrigo)* permit camping on forestry land; one then has access to the sanitary facilities.

Caniçal

The fishing village Caniçal lies at the eastern tip of the island, separated from Machico by 9 kilometres (5½ miles) and a tunnel. The landscape here is flatter and the vegetation more sparse than around Machico. Caniçal attained its special quality by virtue of its remoteness and the fact that access via the tunnel was made possible only fairly recently. Before the tunnel was built, Caniçal could only be reached by ship or on foot over the mountains. Adding to its unique character is its history as an important whaling station.

This village has been able to preserve some of its original atmosphere, especially in the old town centre with its simple church and village square, colourful boats in the harbour, and quaint seafood restaurants.

Between Caniçal and the easternmost point, *Ponta de São Lourenço,* a toll-free zone has recently been established, intended to attract foreign businesses. Unfortunately, the new construction activity is destroying the landscape and some of the hiking trails.

Caniçal / **Sights**

One should not miss a visit to the *Whaling Museum,* the *Museu da Baleia,* near the wharf. It was opened to the public in the Spring of 1990 and is part of the island's meanwhile active nature conservation programme. Nature conservation does not have a long history here. Caniçal was the location of Madeira's whaling station and whale processing plant, in operation from 1941 to 1981. This station was directed by Senhor Eleutério Reis, a whaler from the Azores. Resulting from the Washington Endangered Species Act, member nations, including Portugal, were no longer allowed to export sperm whale products as of 1981. Whaling was stopped immediately, and in cooperation with the Society for the Protection of Marine Mammals, an area of 200,000 square kilometres (78,000 square miles) surrounding Madeira was set aside in 1985 as a national park for marine mammals. At the museum there is a life-size, 13-metre-long (43 feet) cross-section of a sperm whale as well as a whaling boat, which appears very small by comparison. The simple equipment shows that the whale hunters did not use modern, 20th-century technology, but rather relied on hand-held harpoons and lances and the experience of generations of whalers. In addition, an extensive collection of pictures, photographs, and films provide important and interesting facts on whaling, whale biology, and the necessity of nature conservation. One would like to believe that scrimshaw and trophies made of whale bones and teeth are as much a part of the past as whaling itself. Thus, it comes as an even greater shock to see the large array of such items (although they are said to be made from leftover supplies) proudly presented by souvenir sellers in the village and on Ponta de São Lourenço.

The Whales

Here, chiefly sperm whales were hunted and processed in the plant. Taxonomically, they belong to the toothed whales together with white whales, killer whales, narwhals, and the various dolphins. A sperm whale bull can reach up to 18 metres (60 feet) in length, while the cows are on average 11 metres (36 feet) long. The rectangular head comprises up almost one-third of body length, with no distinct external division from the rest of the body. Likewise, the lower jaw is long but very narrow and studded with conical teeth. They feed mostly on squid. Sperm whales are indisputably the best divers among whales in general; they can dive to depths of up to 1,000 metres (3,270 feet) and remain submerged for an hour at a time before having to surface to "catch their breath."

Sperm whales exhibit very highly developed social behaviour, live in fairly large groups (at least the cows, their offspring, and younger whales), and can communicate acoustically with one another over hundreds of miles. Young whales have a long childhood and are nursed for one or two years with the mother's very nutritious milk. As juveniles, they go through so-called whale schools; that is, the regular gatherings of young and old animals. Body contact is in these situations an important medium. Differentiated social behaviour, long learning phases during youth, and the ability to communicate are characteristics of higher intelligence typical among all toothed-whale species. Well-known examples are the famous "Flipper" and other dolphins, or gentle killer whales (orcas).

Whaling was practised as early as the 16th century because these leviathans were the source of many valuable raw materials such as fats and oils for use in medicine and industry, bones and meat for food, fodder, fertiliser, ambergris for scents and pharmaceuticals, other hormones and, last but not least, whale-liver oil rich in vitamin D.

Spermaceti is a delicate mixture of chemicals stored in massive quantities in the sperm whale's head, and no one knows the actual function of this substance in and for the whale itself. It possibly plays a role in sonar transmission and reception or perhaps in buoyancy regulation through density changes. Meanwhile, it is not difficult to produce synthetic substitutes or find natural alternatives for whale products. It is not for this reason alone has the time long since come to protect these wonders of the ocean and research their natural environment.

The national park for marine mammals in the waters surrounding Madeira is a step in the right direction. For the survival of many sea creatures, an expansion of park territory to include the Azores and Canary Islands is urgently needed. The southern half of the Desertas Islands has quite recently been placed under complete protection. It is hoped that the archipelago's monk seals will thus be given the chance to regenerate completely. Their numbers had been reduced to 8 individuals, now there are 12; the cause of their near extinction was irresponsible dynamite fishing, which destroyed their basis of existence and food supply. The Portuguese environmental protection organisation BIOS is headquartered in Caniçal, and has posted guards on the Desertas to ensure that the seals' peace and quiet, essential for their survival, is not disturbed.

It is of utmost importance to provide the inhabitants of the seas, including sea birds, with the protection they require to recover in numbers and maintain species diversity (→*Animals and Wildlife*).

Caniçal / **Practical Information**

Accommodation: "Residençal Prainha Sol" lies at the entrance to town on the main street toward São Lourenço (with restaurant).

Festivals: The festival of *Nossa Senhora da Piedade* (Our Lady of Piety) takes place on the third Sunday in September. A procession of boats brings the icon of *Nossa Senhora* beginning at the Nossa Senhora Chapel on Monte Gordo, past the island's only true swimming beach (Prainha) to Caniçal's parish church and back again on the same route. Naturally, the boats are festively decorated, and the Madeirans take advantage of this religious occasion to put on a real folk festival.

General: On ER 101-3 above the centre of town, one will find all the necessities, such as the bank, post office, restaurants, a supermarket, and the Centro de Saúde.

Swimming: The only, tiny beach on Madeira, called *Prainha* in Portuguese, has black sand and is situated on a small bay.

Transportation: Bus no. 113 serves this region with a route from Funchal through Santa Cruz and Machico. It operates 8 to 12 times daily depending on day of the week. The trip lasts around 1½ hours

Caniço

Caniço is a lively little place that, thanks to its proximity to Funchal, always attracts many visitors; yet it has managed to maintain its village atmosphere. Caniço is one of the island's oldest settlements, whose parish was founded back in 1440. The word "Caniço" means reed or rush, which are said to have thrived in great numbers here at the time the area was settled. The dominant feature of the village is the little plaza with church and a park, around which all the necessary establishments are clustered such as restaurants, cafés, and a supermarket. The stately villas and quintas indicate that this is the country retreat of Funchal's affluent. Caniço's importance in tourism is growing thanks to *Reis Magos* and *Caniço de Baixo,* where holiday centres have either already been established or are just being completed, for instance, the freshly renovated *Quinta Splendida,* which houses a first-class restaurant and stylish hotel.

Caniço / **Practical Information**

Accommodation: "Residencial A Lareira," (double room: 5000$00) with restaurant, Sítio da Vargem, Tel: 93 32 84, 9125 Caniço, located to the right of the church. The "Quinta Splendida" has five exclusive suites and double rooms in a quinta dating back to the past (19,500$00 to 24,000$00). The quinta was purchased and renovated by two Swiss, Giancarlo Bertoli and Gianluigi Rezzonico. Bertoli is a sculptor and antiquarian, Rezzonico a painter, whose works are also on display in the villa (they are also for sale). On the quinta's freshly landscaped, well-tended grounds, another holiday apartment complex with 45 units is under construction. In the quinta, Bertoli and Rezzonico want to create a holiday residence with a very personal style — a union of art and life, which they have succeeded in doing at equally artistic prices.

"Caniço de Baixo": This holiday resort with its hotels, restaurants, and cafés is not far from Caniço and lies directly on the ocean. It is chiefly the German visitors who spend their holidays here. The hotels offer a comprehensive recreational programme, and organise excursions and hikes. A small, rocky beach provides the opportunity for a swim in the Atlantic. To rent studios, apartments, and rooms, contact Anton Sommer, Caniço de Baixo, Tel: 93 22 19, 93 23 85, or 93 25 43.

"Reis Magos": Where once the fishing boats came ashore from the Desertas with their catches, there is now a holiday resort with all the restaurants, shopping centres, and sports and recreation facilities one has come to expect.

Banks: The bank is at the centre of town next to the church, open 8:30 am to 3 pm.

Medical Care: The *Centro de Saúde* is located to the right of the church.

Post Office: The post office is on the same street as "Residencial A Lareira," and is open from 9 am to 12:30 pm and 2 to 6 pm.

Restaurants: Centrally located next to the church, one will find the restaurant "O Vidro," which is also a meeting place for local residents. One can also dine at the restaurant in "Residencial A Lareira," on the right by the church. One can dine in the finest ambience (with prices to match), choosing from a menu that changes daily at the restaurant in "Quinta Splendida," Sítio da Vargem, Caniço, Tel: 93 20 27.

Shopping: A modest shopping centre and the Supermercado Chá, also adjacent to the church, cover the basic needs for which an extra trip to Funchal would be too far.

Swimming: The large hotels (→*Accommodations*) all have pools, as does Caniço de Baixo by the sea.

Transportation: Busses no. 2 (toward Assomada), 23 (Machico), and 113 (Caniçal); travel time is approximately 40 minutes.

Car Rental

The internationally known car rental firms have branches on Madeira, as do the Portuguese companies. For the most part, their main offices are located in Funchal; nearly all have representatives at the airport and some in Machico, Caniço de Baixo, and on Porto Santo. Ask about booking in advance at your travel agency at home. It is usually worthwhile to inquire about discount rates and special offers. For example, rates for a Ford Fiesta for one day and for one week are as follows:

Rental for one day costs about 7200$00, including insurance and tax; one week is around 45,500$00, including everything. There are also different rates for one to three or four days and for six or more days. Luggage racks and car seats for children may be rented with the car upon request. Booking in advance is recommended.

Prices listed here are given as guidelines; during the peak season they may be somewhat higher, special offers may include discounts of 10 to 20%.

Depending on the company, one must be either 21 or 23 years old to rent a car and have had a valid driving licence for at least one year or a driving licence and comparable driving experience. Driving in Funchal and between towns does in fact require some getting used to and quite a bit of concentration.

Addresses:

Atlantic, Hotel "Belo Sol," Caminho Velho da Ajuda, 9000 Funchal, Tel: 76 52 08, Telex: 72 521, Fax: 6 17 12; Hotel "Duas Torres," Tel: 2 28 80, 3 00 64; airport 6 17 12/2; Av. Vieira de Castro, 9400 Porto Santo, Tel: 98 26 83, Telex: 72 231.

Avis, Largo António Nobre 164, 9000 Funchal, Tel: 2 54 95 or 2 25 46; airport, Tel: 5 23 92, Telex: 72 101.

Budget, Hotel "Duas Torres," Estrada Monumental 239, 9000 Funchal, Tel: 2 56 19 or 3 25 08; Centro Comercial Matur-Machico, Tel: 96 23 83 or 96 23 05, Telex: 72 345 BRAC-P.

Europcar, Estrada Monumental, Funchal, Tel: 5 37 33, open daily from 7:00 am to midnight.

Hertz, Rua Ivens 12, 9000 Funchal, Tel: 2 60 26; Av. do Infante (across from the Casino Park Hotel), 9000 Funchal, Tel: 4 40 64; airport, Tel: 52 23 60, Telex: 7 23 14. In addition, there are "Atlas," "Garagem Santiago," "Horizonte," "Lidorent," "Moinho," and "Rodavante."

Carapuça

These caps of sheep's wool with the bobble and ear flaps are called "carapuça" or "barrete." The carapuças of each region have their own colours, shapes, and bobbles. Men wear these caps any time of day. The original caps are brown and naturally coloured; children and tourists prefer the brightly coloured ones.

Children

Most Portuguese are very open and friendly toward children, and take them along to restaurants and cafés or even out for an evening with the whole family. Madeira is, however, not very well suited for younger children, since beaches on which they can play are virtually nonexistent and during rough weather, the crossing to Porto Santo can be quite hard on a small child (→*Porto Santo*).

Climate

Madeira is, for most of the year, under the influence of the northeasterly trade winds that blow constant good weather across from the subtropical high-pressure regions in the southwest. With an Azores high pressure area, the island enjoys clear blue skies, sunshine and calm seas.

During the winter, the weather is frequently influenced by low pressure areas from the far north: heavy clouds, falling temperatures and abundant precipitation. In spite of this, the winters here are especially mild. Average temperatures of 16 °C (61 °F) in winter and 22 °C (72 °F) in summer, lack of large daily temperature swings, and moderate levels of humidity make Madeira's climate very mild and pleasant. From August to September, though, the days can be very hot and humid.

Average temperatures or rainfall, however, do not say much about local weather conditions, which vary considerably from place to place on Madeira. Fundamental differences distinguish the north side of the island from the south. The north is characterised by heavy precipitation. In contrast, the south has several months of drought in summer (May to September), low yearly rainfall (maximum in November), more hours of sun, and temperatures between a minimum of 10 °C (50 °F) and a maximum of 30 °C (86 °F). This applies only to lower-lying regions, that is, mainly to coastal areas.

High plateaus and peaks often lie above the clouds and are thus drier and exposed to greater temperature extremes. Wintry frost and snow on the picos — when Funchal enjoys relatively summery temperatures — impressively illustrate the kind of weather conditions possible on Madeira. Porto Santo is flatter and smaller, so that Atlantic weather can simply sweep across the island. Rain showers seldom last longer than ten minutes, and in summer, sunshine is nearly guaranteed.

Climate Table

	Funchal			Porto Moniz			Porto Santo		
	1	2	3	1	2	3	1	2	3
January	16 (61)	116 (4.6)	13	11 (52)	22 (0.9)	16	16 (61)	65 (2.6)	14
February	16 (61)	95 (3.7)	11	10 (50)	192 (7.6)	16	15 (59)	49 (1.9)	12
March	16 (61)	67 (2.6)	11	11 (52)	132 (5.2)	13	16 (61)	145 (5.7)	11
April	16 (61)	39 (1.5)	7	11 (52)	87 (3.4)	12	16 (61)	21 (0.8)	8
May	18 (65)	16 (0.6)	4	12 (54)	86 (3.4)	11	18 (65)	12 (0.5)	6
June	19 (67)	11 (0.4)	3	14 (58)	66 (2.6)	12	20 (68)	6 (0.2)	5
July	21 (70)	3 (0.1)	1	16 (61)	27 (1.1)	6	21 (70)	3 (0.1)	4
August	22 (72)	4 (0.2)	1	17 (63)	46 (1.8)	6	22 (72)	6 (0.2)	4
September	22 (72)	20 (0.8)	5	17 (63)	102 (4.0)	11	22 (72)	14 (0.6)	6
October	21 (70)	73 (2.9)	10	16 (61)	182 (7.2)	16	21 (61)	48 (1.9)	11
November	18 (65)	103 (4.1)	11	13 (56)	220 (8.7)	18	18 (65)	52 (2.0)	13
December	16 (61)	92 (3.6)	13	11 (52)	66 (2.6)	17	16 (61)	60 (2.4)	15

1 average monthly temperature in °C (°F)
2 precipitation in mm (inches)
3 rainy days

Not at all uncommon: a bank of clouds hovers below the mountain peaks

Clothing

Light clothing is sufficient in summer; at the most, one will need a sweater or light jacket for the cooler evening hours. During the rest of the year and on the north coast, always bring an umbrella, raincoat, and warm jacket. For hiking, good walking shoes or hiking boots and rain gear are essential. When visiting churches, one should dress appropriately in order not to offend the very religious Portuguese's sense of piety and decency.

Conduct

Madeira is conservative, very religious, and patriarchal; its people value politeness and hospitality highly. Visitors should remember they are guests and behave accordingly, i.e., not enter churches when dressed for swimming or sunbathing and not sunbathe or swim nude. One should accept local customs and not put on an air of superiority if, for instance, one finds the busses at home far better than these old clunkers. The bus drivers are amazingly skillful when driving in the mountains: what bus driver at home could back a fully-loaded bus for 100 metres along a road no wider than his vehicle to let oncoming traffic pass without losing his nerve?

Credit Cards →Currency

Crime

The crime rate on Madeira is quite low, but is growing proportionally with tourism. In case of theft, it is best to inform the hotel reception, who will then notify the police, since police often speak no foreign languages (→Police). The best prevention is, of course, to keep one's eyes open and avoid situations conducive to theft, such as leaving valuables unguarded. One should take only the most necessary valuables along on holiday, and deposit them in the hotel safe when not in use.

Cuisine

The cuisine on Madeira is, with regional specialities, very similar to that of Portugal. The island's residents, of course, eat a lot of seafood. The deep-sea fish "Espada" is a typical dish served in endless variations. Espada filet can be ordered nearly everywhere; swordfish is especially tasty when served with a fried banana. Freshly grilled, plate-sized tuna filet steaks are on the menu daily during the tuna fishing season. Sticklebacks, rosefish, sardines, and sea bass can be ordered in seafood restaurants. Speciality restaurants occasionally offer morays, which are high in price. Catching morays is very difficult and somewhat dangerous because they live in caves and their bite is poisonous. Trout from the fisheries in Ribeiro Frio are on the menu from time to time. Typically Portuguese is the preference for bacalhau, the dried and salted cod for which there are more than 300 recipes. Fish stew is called "caldeirada."

Small snails, pulled out of their shells with a pin, are a popular hors d'oeuvre ("lapas"). Madeira has few shellfish, both in the sea surrounding the island and on the menu.

Meats include, aside from the internationally common steaks and chops, two typically Madeiran and ubiquitous dishes. "Espetada" (not to be confused with "Espada," a fish) is a kind of shish kebab grilled over an open fire. The meat obtains a special aroma when skewered on laurel twigs ("espetada de louro"). Earlier, one grilled espetada oneself; today, the long iron skewers rubbed with laurel are either hung from the ceiling or fastened to stands on the table. "Carne de vinhos e alhos" is an especially savoury meat dish. Pork is marinated for several days in a mixture of wine, garlic, laurel, and spices, and is then fried in lard. A good first course is tomato and onion soup ("sopa de tomate e cebola/com ovo"); upon request mixed with egg, it's a meal in itself for lighter appetites. "Caldo verde" is a very tasty kale soup for which potatoes are pureed and the kale grated into fine strips.

"Milho frito" is a common side-dish of fried corn meal dough, reminiscent of croquettes. (The corn is boiled in saltwater with strips of cabbage and a bit of lard or margarine for about an hour until it has the consistency of porridge. It is then spooned onto a plate to cool. The cooled plateful is cut into quarters and fried until crisp.)

Typical local cuisine does not emphasise vegetables; imaginative salads can hardly be found in the more affordable restaurants.

Most restaurants serve international cuisine in addition to Madeiran specialties. In Funchal, there are Chinese, Belgian, and Italian restaurants (→Funchal/Cuisine). At cake shops, one will notice a small, round, brown cake similar to gingerbread and covered with almonds. This is "bolo de mel," or honey cake made of sugar cane syrup and fruit. It keeps for up to a year if made well. At Christmas, it is commonly sent to relatives overseas.

"Bolo de caco" is not actually cake, as the name would lead one to believe ("bolo" means cake), but rather a round bread made with yams.

Beverages

The local beer is called Coral. Beer from the Portuguese mainland and foreign imports are also served.

Locally produced table wine is, unfortunately, almost nonexistent since most of the harvest is used to produce Madeira Wine.

Most of the table wines come from Portugal itself and cost upwards of 800$00 per bottle. "Vinho Verde" is a red or white wine fermented from unripened grapes, which give it its light, tingly flavour. Madeira Wine is, of course, an integral part of dining in style: for every course there is an appropriate Madeira (→Wine).

The sugar cane industry may no longer play such a dominant role on the archipelago as it did during its heyday producing "white gold," (→History) but sugar cane schnapps is as popular as ever among the Madeirans. This "aguardente de cana de açucar" is a superb after-dinner drink. "Poncha" is a cocktail of sugar cane schnapps, honey, and lemon. The mixture is stirred with a wooden swizzle stick until thinned. Other special drinks include various fruit liqueurs, such as cherry, maracuja, and banana.

Coffee is celebrated as an indispensable part of the culture in the numerous cafés. A "café" or "bica" is a small, strong espresso enjoyed at all hours of the day and night. An espresso with a dollop of whipped cream is called "café com natas." A "galão" is café au lait in a water glass. Café au lait in a medium-sized cup is a "chinesa" — a Chinese. ("Chinesa" is known only on Madeira.) Café au lait in a small espresso cup is known as a "garoto." An espresso cut with water is called "carioca." The closest thing to a normal cup of coffee is a "café grande."

Restaurants, Cafés, Snack Bars, Pastelarias

As a rule, the Portuguese get together in cafés instead of at home. People of all ages go to cafés. Waiters and waitresses are attentive and the service is relatively fast. If the service is good, round up for the tip; if not, let it be. Many cafés call themselves snack bars, although snacks are available most everywhere. "Tosta mista" is toasted white bread with ham and/or cheese. "Torrada" consists of two pieces of white toast with salted butter cut into strips. Assorted sandwiches on white bread or rolls are called "sandes." The Portuguese are more interested in good service, good prices, and good (that is, strong) coffee when choosing a favourite café than in appearances. If one is uncertain about which café has good service and decent prices, have a look at where the Madeirans are sitting. This is especially true of the sidewalk cafés on the quays in Funchal; there are some "tourist traps" among them.

Pastelarias are cafés with a large selection of very tasty cakes.

In less expensive restaurants, one can often find very economically-priced lunches (from about 450$00), since many Madeirans eat out during their midday break. Take-away or fast-food chains have not (yet) come to Madeira.

Students at the hotel-management school on Madeira prepare culinary delights and serve the guests with professionalism and style *(→Quintas)*. The spectrum of eating establishments on the island is astounding: one finds everything from small, family owned and operated restaurants to fine dining in a four-star hotel complete with an award-winning chef *(→individual entries)*.

Lunch is served from 12 to 3 pm, dinner from 7 to 10 or 11 pm. Breakfast is not very important to the Portuguese, and "continental breakfast" is served only in those cafés frequented by tourists, where visitors from England and America will not have to forego bacon and eggs even while on holiday. The Portuguese normally eat only sparingly in the morning and stop briefly at one of the many cafés for a wake-up "bica."

Curral das Freiras

The "Valley of Nuns," as the name translates, is an area of interesting landscapes whose geology is somewhat puzzling. The valley is a nearly closed basin with walls up to 500 metres (1,635 feet) high *(→Geology)*. The only outlet is the narrow valley of Ribeira do Curral, which flows into the sea at Vitório. The valley got its name from the nuns that fled the Santa Clara convent to hide here during pirate attacks in the 16th and 17th centuries. Geologically, it could be a collapsed crater or a product of erosion.

The little village can only be reached by climbing 900 stairs from the valley floor or from above along the road ER 107, which winds through two tunnels and several curves before coming to the village. By car, one can take a side trip to Eira do Serrado and from there, walk to Pico do Serrado (15 minutes) for a view down into the Curral and of the island's highest peaks in the background. Definitely worth seeing!

The village of Curral das Freiras is small enough that one can see all of it during a short walk. Bus no. 81 stops at the plaza above the church where bars, small shops, and souvenir stands are also found.

From Corticeiras, one can hike to the valley of nuns *(→Hiking),* or coming from Funchal, along the Levada do Curral. The latter trail should only be taken by experienced hikers. The hike from Corticeiras is strenuous, but not dangerous in dry weather.

In August, the festival of *Nossa Senhora do Livramento* and in September the chestnut festival are celebrated.

→Holidays and Celebrations

Currency

Madeira's currency is the Portuguese escudo. There are 1, 2½, 5, 10, 20, 50, 100, and 200 escudo coins, and notes of 100, 500, 1000, 5000, and 10,000 escudos. 1 escudo consists of 100 centavos. (Centavos have, however, been taken out of circulation.)

At the moment, two different 1000-escudo bills are in circulation; both are valid. On price tags and signs, the escudo is abbreviated with a dollar sign. Left of the dollar sign is the escudo amount, right the centavos. 5000 escudos is officially written 5000$00.

Just as in Portugal, traveller's cheques and Eurocheques are accepted on Madeira. It is a good idea to cash them at a bank, however, since many shops bear a great mistrust for Eurocheques. Credit cards like Eurocard, Visa, American Express, and Mastercard are accepted in finer restaurants and tourist shops and hotels. A sign at the door often lists which cards are taken. A Eurocheque can be written out for as much as 30,000$00 escudos. Eurocheque cards can be used to obtain cash at the "Multibanco" automated cash machines; instructions are also given in English.

Inflation is high in Portugal, making it impossible to give a fixed rate of exchange. Approximately, £1 = 258$00, $1.00 = 138$00; 100$00 = £0.39 and $0.75. Exchanging money on Madeira is much less expensive than at home; thus, one should exchange only a small sum to escudos before arriving on Madeira.

The fee for cashing traveller's cheques at some banks can be as high as 818$00 (about £3 or $6) for one transaction; the Turismo bureau (→ *Tourist Information*) and *Montepio Geral* bank charge "only" 545$00.

There is no fee for exchanging cash up to 5,000$00 per transaction (about £20 or $38); a fee of 500$00 is charged for higher sums. In Funchal, there are automated machines where one can exchange money, but fees range from 100$00 to 300$00. At post offices, one can withdraw up to 30,000$00 a day if one has a postal account. Exchange rates at the post office are usually slightly less favourable than at banks (→ *Postal System*).

Customs Regulations

The following may be brought into Portugal duty-free:

300 cigarettes or 150 cigarillos or 75 cigars or 400 grams tobacco; 1.5 litres of alcoholic beverages of up to 22% or 3 litres of alcoholic beverages of over 22% or 5 litres of wine; 75 grams of perfume; 1000 grams of coffee or 400 grams of coffee extract; 200 grams of tea or 80 grams tea extract. Medications may be brought in for personal use. There is no limit on currency and cheques.

One is allowed to take out duty-free:

Up to 100,000$00 per person per trip, foreign currencies with a value of up to 500,000$00; there is no limit to other means of payment (cheques etc.). Travellers under 17 years of age may bring in neither tobacco products nor alcoholic beverages.

Discounts

Students with international student identification are seldom eligible for discounts in museums. Night life is also rarely subject to discounted prices, being that admission is very inexpensive or even free of charge. Children from 12 to 14 years of age can receive a discount on bus tours or organised excursions of up to 50%.

Economy

Madeira is a highly agricultural island with no mineral resources of any kind. It has almost no industry, except one paper and one cigarette factory which produces the local brands "Bingo" and "Santa Maria." The free-trade zone near Caniçal is intended to attract foreign businesses to Madeira. Broadly outlined, Madeira's economy is based one third on the currencies from emigrants, one third on tourism, and one third on the traditional Madeiran occupations such as farming, wine production, fishing, embroidery, and basket weaving. Agriculture has always been a hard way to make a living on Madeira, and in the course of history it has been subject to a number of catastrophes (collapse of sugar exports, grapevine diseases →*History, Agriculture*). Resulting from Portugal's membership in the EC, banana exports will decline in the near future since the small Madeiran bananas cannot compete with the larger, cheaper fruits from South America. Instead, the EC subsidises the production of the excellent Madeira Wine, for which demand always exceeds supply due to the small size of the vineyards. Many farmers are shifting from banana crops to growing flowers, which have good export chances. Tourism is an important source of income, creating jobs for young Madeirans as well. Overpopulation and unemployment have long been Madeira's biggest problems. Many Madeirans emigrate to Venezuela, South Africa, Europe, Australia, and the United States. The money they earn abroad is an important component of Madeira's economy. Many return years later and invest their earnings in restaurants, hotels, and other businesses in the service sector. The living standards are, however, still very low. The legal minimum wage is 41,000$00 a month, about $280 or £160. The cost of living is, however, not much lower than in England or the US, and new apartments are actually more expensive. This leads to crowded living quarters, forcing many Madeirans to work two or more jobs at once. Such difficulties can only be dealt with when families stay together and help each other make ends meet.

Electricity

The power supply system delivers 220 volts and the outlets are the same as in the rest of Europe. Visitors from outside Europe may need an adaptor to use their electrical appliances.

Embassies

American Embassy: Avenida das Foçras Armadas, 1600 Lisbon, Tel: 726 66 00.
Australian Embassy: Avenida da Liberdade 244, 1200 Lisbon, Tel: 003511/52 33 50.
British Embassy: São-Domingos-Lapa 37, 1200 Lisbon, Tel: 66 11 91.

Embroidery

Embroidery as an industry has been practised on Madeira only since the mid 19th century. An Englishwoman, Mrs. Phelps, introduced it as a means for Madeiran women to earn extra money. She then had their products exported to Victorian England. In the 19th century, Madeirans were in great need of extra income, since wine trading — the main industry at the time — declined drastically as a result of a leaf disease and a grape-aphid plague (→*Wine/History*). Trade in embroidery flourished. During the world wars and economic crises, however, export fell off markedly, on the one hand because tourism declined and on the other, because this luxury item could not be sold. Today, embroidered wares are as much a part of Madeira as the wine. Most is produced by home workers, but there are also factories and in Machico even an embroidery school *(→Machico)*, which also offers tours. Workers are paid by the stitch, and although the minimum wage is set by law, this work is among the most underpaid and hardest on the island. The quality is controlled by the "Instituto do Bordado, Tapeçaria e Artesanato" (Institute of Embroidery, Tapestry, and Crafts), which attaches a quality seal and small metal tags that one should look for when purchasing embroidered work. The prices in shops are set, and one can bargain only with those who sell their home-produced goods on the street; here, of course, there is no quality control. In Funchal one can tour some of the factories which, like the wineries, have shops. The Madeirans named a street after Mrs. Phelps.

Emergencies

The emergency number is 115 on Madeira and Porto Santo and in all of Portugal for police and ambulance. In the case of a traffic accident, notify the car rental company and police.

Encumeada

The *Boca da Encumeada* is 1,007 metres (3,293 feet) high and lies off of ER 104, the road connecting the north and south of Madeira. When the weather is clear, one has a fascinating view over the island with São Vicente in the north and Ribeira Brava in the south. To and from Encumeada Pass, there are a number of different hikes recommended only for sure-footed, experienced hikers when the weather is good and dry. In the fog or rain, Encumeada becomes one of Madeira's most inhospitable spots. At this elevation, there is more ground fog and rain than on the coast, where at the same time, much more pleasant weather can be found. A little bar provides for refreshments or, should the weather be wet and cold, mixes a *Poncha (→Cuisine)* with a punch!

About another kilometre farther towards São Vicente, a shady picnic spot in a small grove provides the ideal opportunity for a longer stop (with a place to grill).

Entertainment

Evening entertainment is concentrated in Funchal. In the smaller towns and villages, only the first-class hotels have every sort of entertainment programme. In Funchal, one can live it up in bars, discos, and Madeira's casino. The cinemas show current, international films in their original language with Portuguese subtitles. The large hotels have quite a range of evening activities, e.g. folklore, dance, or disco evenings.

(→Theatre)

Estreito de Câmara de Lobos

Estreito de Câmara de Lobos lies surrounded by vineyards about 5 km (3 miles) north of Câmara de Lobos and a few metres higher, so that one has a lovely view of the sea, the coastline, and Cabo Girão. The road to Estreito is steep and winding and traffic frequently jams because there is no place to overtake slow vehicles. At the village square, one should not miss visiting the lovely church with blue and white tiles, dark pews and a magnificently coloured wooden ceiling. There are also a few bars, restaurants, and shops at the square. Seen from the church portal, the little market hall is located to the left of the filling station. Going north from the church along the street that leads to the right, one finds a supermarket, a pastelaria, and the Centro de Saúde. On the street leading to the left, there is a bank, post office, and junk shops. Continuing straight ahead on this street, one passes the *Nossa Senhora da Graça Chapel* and comes to the Levada do Norte, along which one can hike. The walk to *Boca dos Namorados* follows the road to Corticeiras and reaches its destination about a quarter of the way to Curral das Freiras. The route is rather strenuous, but one is rewarded by a spectacular view of the Curral.

In Estreito and its fertile vicinity, chestnuts, nuts, cherries, and especially good grapes thrive. The grape harvest is celebrated in September with a big festival, followed by folklore performances.

The pastelaria "Sto. António" down on the main street toward Ribeira Brava is a good, inexpensive restaurant.

The **doctor and pharmacy** are located at the entrance to town, in front of the church to the left.

Excursions

Madeira's main attraction is its landscape, best discovered on excursions. With a rental car, one will gain a very individual impression of the island, but one can also get almost everywhere by bus. In Funchal's immediate vicinity, travelling by bus is relatively simple and convenient. However, the further from the city one wants to go, the less frequent the bus connections become. Organised tours by coach or simply by taxi are other alternatives for getting to know the island. A wide variety of excursions by ship or plane are also available.

Speed of travel is quite slow as a result of the poor, narrow and winding streets and roads (30-50 km/h or 18-30 mph). Bus lines are in operation to nearly all the points of interest, but the routes were planned for getting Madeirans to and from work and not for tourism. Thus, departure times are often in the early morning or evening.

Suggested excursions are listed according to distance and/or the time needed to enjoy a leisurely visit to the region or town

Excursions / **Short Excursions by Car/Bus**

Suggested short trips are to: Monte, Camacha, Câmara de Lobos, Cabo Girão, the botanic garden, and Blandy's Garden (Quinta Palheiro Ferreiro). For details, like bus connections, see →*individual entries.*

Excursions / **Day Trips by Car/Bus**

Funchal — Pico do Arieiro — Pico Ruivo

A hike from Madeira's second highest peak to the highest, Pico Ruivo, is one of the most unforgettable experiences this island has to offer. From every bend in the trail, the mountains present new vistas of valleys and ravines. The trail is strenuous but safe.

→*Hiking, Pico do Arieiro, Pico Ruivo*

Funchal — Ribeira Brava — Encumeada — São Vicente

Up to Câmara de Lobos the road is very busy, and driving in the morning, especially at rush hour (8 to 9 o'clock), is anything but a pleasure. One shouldn't become discouraged, though; after taking a short break in the town of Ribeira Brava (→*Ribeira Brava)* one will see that the landscape is just beginning to get interesting. The road over the pass, whose highest point is Encumeada (→*Encumeada),* crosses a bizarre mountain landscape that is still intensely farmed despite its topography. When the weather is clear, one has a beautiful view from Encumeada over the north and south sides of the island. Descending from the pass, the countryside becomes greener and more fertile. There are a number of lovely *Miradouros* (scenic outlooks) and picnic spots on this stretch of road.

Funchal — Machico — Caniçal — São Lourenço

On the way to Machico, Caniço and Santa Cruz (→*Caniço, Santa Cruz)* are worth stopping for a short visit. Machico is, after Funchal, the second largest and liveliest city on Madeira and represents a milestone in the island's history (→*History, Machico).* The little fishing village of Caniçal became accessible by motor vehicle only a few years ago. Up until recently, there was a whaling station here; now there is a whaling museum (→*Caniçal).* The easternmost point of Madeira, Ponta de São Lourenço, is a lovely region for walking and hiking. Madeira's only sand beach, Prainha, is also located here.

→*Ponta de São Lourenço*

Funchal — Ribeira Brava — Canhas — Paúl da Serra — Rabaçal

The uninhabited, barren plateau Paúl da Serra (→*Paúl da Serra)* stands in marked contrast to the island's lush green hillsides with their picturesque terraced fields and scattered houses. The mountains surrounding the plateau are covered with heather, gorse, and laurel forests. Rabaçal lies in one of the valleys, which seems

like another world after leaving the spartan landscape of the Paúl: the pastoral valley with its rushing streams and waterfalls is very inviting for hikers and pic-nickers.
→*Rabaçal*

Funchal — Monte — Ribeiro Frio — Faial — (Santana) — Camacha
The trout hatchery in Ribeiro Frio is in an idyllic spot worth visiting, and pleasant walks in the vicinity are possible (→*Ribeiro Frio*). In Faial, one can have an ex-cellent lunch, and a short side trip to Santana for a look at the picturesque straw houses is a must (→*Santana, Faial*). From →*Portela* there is an excellent view of the northern coast when the weather is good. Camacha is the centre of the wicker industry. In addition to souvenirs, there is a fine view of the southern coast.

Funchal — Camacha — Santo da Serra — Machico
The only golf course on Madeira is near Santo da Serra. The woods around this village and the Quinta do Santo (where there is a small zoo) are good opportunities for a long stroll (→*Santo da Serra*).
→*Camacha, Machico*

Funchal — Ribeira Brava — São Vicente — Santana — Porto da Cruz — Machico — Funchal
This is the more extensive eastern tour for people with limited time since it in-cludes many of Madeira's attractions in one trip: Encumeada Pass, the tranquil São Vicente, the cottages of Santana, and historical Machico.

Excursions / **Overnight Excursions**
Porto Moniz
Although one can visit Madeira's northernmost town in a day, staying the night is recommended. The trip is rather lengthy and tiring; thus, it is better to plan the return trip the next day. One should be sure to go for a swim in Porto Moniz's natural swimming pool (→*Porto Moniz*). The following briefly describe the three routes to Porto Moniz:

Funchal — Ribeira Brava — Calheta — Ponta do Pargo — Porto Moniz
For the driver, this route is the most demanding due to the poor, winding roads, but it is certainly one of the most beautiful and diverse in terms of scenic land-scapes. Some of the west-coast villages are still "untouched," that is, road ac-cess was built only a few years ago and the settlements therefore appear unspoil-ed. Tourist facilities, such as restaurants, cafés, and hotels are very rare along this route.

Funchal — Ribeira Brava — São Vicente — Seixal — Porto Moniz
The road between São Vicente and Porto Moniz is among the most impressive on the entire island: a narrow cobblestone road weaves its way along the coast, passing a number of plummeting waterfalls, one of which pours directly over the road into the sea. Delightful!

Funchal — Ribeira Brava — Canhas — Paúl da Serra — Porto Moniz
This is the second shortest route to Porto Moniz after the one through São Vicente and Seixal. Road conditions are good.

Excursions / **Excursions by Coach**
Tours of the island offered by English or Portuguese tour agencies can be booked through most hotels or at one of the many travel agencies. Most trips last all day, the well-informed tour guides are full of interesting details. Occasionally, a trip will include a short hike or stop at a traditional restaurant or folkloric inn. Depending on the length and content of the trip, prices range from 2500$00 to 6000$00. Tour organisers offer a different tour every weekday, from short excursions to complete tours of the island.

During excursions into the island's interior, one will become acquainted with the bizarre mountain landscape of Madeira

The advantages of coach travel are that someone else does the driving along the bumpy roads; thus, one can enjoy the scenery without having to pay attention to the traffic. The disadvantages of coach travel are that one has a set schedule and the tight itinerary is sometimes rather hectic.

Excursions / **Excursions by Taxi**

As a special service, some taxi drivers offer longer or shorter tours of Funchal or the entire island in English. These tours are highly individualised and flexible, and the tourist benefits from the driver's in-depth local knowledge. With four to six people, the price is very reasonable (for instance, four people pay a total of 7500$00 to 13,000$00 per trip). The price should be agreed upon with the driver before starting the tour. The hotel reception can usually recommend a driver, or one can call the English-speaking taxi driver Herculano Sousa, Tel: 92 21 85 (Camacha) or 93 38 02 (home).

Excursions / **Excursions by Ship**

Some yachts and motor boats offer excursions for tourists. Half- and full-day trips go along the south coast to east or west, depending on wind and weather conditions. These tours usually include a stop for swimming and a snack. Trips to the Desertas or tours by night can be unforgettable experiences. The anchor is dropped off the coast of the Desertas (but not in the south zone, which is a protected area for seals), but going ashore is not allowed since all the islands are nature reserves. With some luck, dolphins might accompany the boat since they enjoy playing in the bow waves. Tour prices vary; to Cabo Girão and back for a half day one pays 2500$00, a full-day trip to the Desertas costs about 6900$00.

Reservations can be made directly at the boat or by phoning a tour organiser (even a few days in advance), or at one of the offices on the quay. The telephone numbers are posted at the sailboat dock.

One can also make the crossing to Porto Santo by catamaran to swim, planning one or several days into one's travel itinerary.

→*Porto Santo*

Excursions/ **Excursions by Plane**

Excursion to Porto Santo (→*Porto Santo*). Recently, weekend trips to the Azores in summer have been introduced. For further information, contact the TUI Travel Agency on Avenida do Mar Street.

→*Travel on Madeira*

Faial

Faial is a small village on the northern coast, which actually has little to offer with the exception of fantastic views and two excellent restaurants. Directly after entering the village (from Porto da Cruz) there are signs for the restaurant "A Chave." When the weather is good, one can dine on the terrace with a view of the village and the ocean. The cuisine is outstanding and the prices are reasonable. "A Chave" is, unfortunately, open only for lunch. The second restaurant is located somewhat outside of Faial on ER 103 toward Lombo de Cima. "Casa de Chá" is a tourist-oriented complex. Its special attraction is a very photogenic reproduction of a "Santana cottage" next to the restaurant. It appears almost more typical of a Santana cottage than the cottages in Santana itself.

The church in Faial is a plain building, supported by donations from natives of Faial now living and working in Venezuela. A plaque inside the church lists the names of donors and sums donated (in Bolivares). In September, the *Festa de Conceição* is celebrated here.

Famous Personalities

This small Atlantic island was always a favourite destination for illustrious visitors. The actress Sarah Bernhardt spent her holidays here, as did Gustav Gründgens (German actor), who even owned a house on Madeira. Winston Churchill especially enjoyed painting scenes of →*Câmara de Lobos,* and the ancestors of American author John dos Passos came from →*Ponta do Sol.* Empress "Sissi" of Austria convalesced from a lung disease in the Quinta Vigia (in 1861) in Funchal, now the government building (→*Quintas).* In the Vicente photographic museum there is still a picture of Empress Elisabeth taken by the Madeiran photographer Vicente, who was thereafter given the titles of Austrian Court Photographer. The daughter of the Brazilian emperor Princess D. Maria Amélia, sought a cure for tuberculosis on Madeira, but unfortunately died a few months after her arrival on the island in 1853. After World War I, Emperor Karl I of Austria went into exile in Funchal. At first, he lived at Reid's, then in a quinta in Monte. He died suddenly of a lung infection in 1922 and, having won the hearts of a great proportion of the Madeiran populace, was buried at the church in Monte. Madeira's geographical position made the island a station for numerous famous seafarers and discoverers such as James Cook and Christopher Columbus (→*Porto Santo/Columbus Museum).*

Ferries →*Travelling on Madeira*

Folklore

Madeira's folklore is rich and colourful. Not only do women in traditional costumes sell flowers, but nearly every village has its own folklore group. These are an integral part of the community and are even popular among young Madeirans; the folklore group is often the only other form of free-time activity apart from the sports clubs. The main annual event occurs in Santana, where singers and dancers continually perform traditional pieces for 24 hours.

→*Santana*

Fruit

The mild, subtropical climate provides ideal conditions for the flourishing and magnificent tropical plants (→Vegetation) but a variety of tropical fruits as well. Many exotic plants were introduced and cultivated here. One should definitely sample the large and colourful selection of fruits at the market. For instance:

Avocados

These dark green, pear-shaped drupes originated in the tropical mountain forests of the Americas. Based on archaeological finds from tombs, the Aztecs were familiar with them as long as 8,000 years ago. This member of the laurel family reaches heights of 20 metres (65 feet) and produces countless small yellow-green flowers in panicles, but only about 1 of 5,000 blossoms matures into fruit. Thanks to its nutty flavour and high fat content (3-30%), there are a variety of ways to serve the fruit: with salt, pepper, oil and vinegar in a salad; on hearty bread with cheese, tomato, plenty of garlic, salt and pepper; with sugar and lemon as a sweet appetiser or dessert, or simply plain with Madeira wine.

Papaya

This large, green, soft fruit is borne at the top of an up to 6-metre-tall (20 feet) greenish tree trunk with lobed, palmate leaves. The tree is intensively cultivated in tropical and subtropical America. The flesh of the fruit is orange and juicy, and tastes similar to apricots and melons; the small, inedible black seeds taste like cress. Papayas are high in vitamins A and C.

Anona or Cherimoya

One simply must try this fruit! The peak harvest season is during winter and early spring, when it can be found in abundance at low prices at markets and every fruit stand. Out of season, the fruits are less common and less tasty. They are fist-sized, heart-shaped, green to brown, and scaly. Their form resembles a gigantic strawberry. Structurally, this is a composite fruit with many small, shiny brown seeds. When the fruit is a little soft, one can spoon out the creamy white, juicy flesh that has as slight aroma of cinnamon. The British call this fruit a custard-apple because of its flavour.

The anona originated in the northern Andes, flourishing in higher mountainous areas. On Madeira, it thrives on the southern coast at elevations of up to 600 metres (1960 feet) and on the northern coast up to 300 metres (980 feet).

Bananas

Bananas originally come from the Indomalaysian region. Arab traders brought them to Africa, where they were given their present name. From there, Portuguese seafarers introduced them to the Canary Islands and Madeira. At the beginning of the 16th century, bananas were brought to South America, where the Indios spread their intensive cultivation.

On Madeira, bananas are cultivated on a large scale, but only for consumption on the island itself and in Portugal. There are two types: the small, yellow-green

Banana ana and the somewhat angular, green-brown silver banana. The former is clearly predominant, since it bears more fruit and is not as difficult to grow and transport. The silver banana is very tasty, but not hardy enough for export (→*Agriculture*).

Maracujá, Passion fruit

On Madeira, this fruit is called *Grenadilla,* which is also widely known for its extraordinarily beautiful blossoms. This type of berry has the size and shape of an egg with a yellow, red or green peel. The plants themselves climb on trellises or other supports and blossom from April to September. Each blossom develops into a fruit; these are harvested from June until September. The fruits are ripe and edible when the outer skin is leathery and firm. This allows for the peel and inedible seeds to be easily removed. On Madeira, a special type of liqueur is produced using this aromatic, sweet yet acidic juice.

Mango

This fruit was already cultivated as early as 2000 B.C. in East India and Burma and then spread from there to other parts of the world. It was once again the Portuguese seafarers who were responsible for the extensive dispersion of this fruit to Africa and Brazil. Mango trees can grow to a height of 30 metres (90 feet)

Exotic fruits thrive in the subtropical climate of Madeira

although on Madeira they rarely reach these dimensions. They also retain their leaves during the entire year. The fruit ripens between September and December and can then be purchased at the marketplaces. A large pit is surrounded by the juicy fruit, rich in vitamin C, A and fructose.

Fruto delicioso

The philodendron belongs to the arum family of plants and is popular house plant. On Madeira, the natural conditions are far more favourable as evidenced by the fact that the philodendron grows in many areas to impressive heights and blooming often. The characteristic large leaves can hardly be overlooked, with their oblong holes and slits in the leaves. The cluster of blossoms is surrounded by a single leaf which is white on the outside and yellow on the inside. A cluster of berries develop from the individual blossoms. During the summer and autumn, these are among the established assortment at the marketplaces, although not available in large quantities.

Medlar

The large medlar trees can often be seen in gardens along the southern coast. The fruit, also called Japanese medlar or loquat, ripen during the first half of the year. The trees grow mainly on the southern portion of Madeira. The small, yellow fruits are very refreshing due to their sweet-sour flavour

Guava

These small, greenish-yellow fruits ripen from the period from autumn to winter on the branches of knotted trees. The berries develop from lovely white blossoms and grow to the size of a table tennis ball. The fruit itself is rich in vitamins and has the flavour similar to that of quince. Jellies and jams are often made from these fruits, but they are also served in their original form. Unfortunately, the numerous seeds distract somewhat from the aromatic flavour.

Fuel

Normal and super cost between 145$00 and 165$00 per litre, diesel runs about 100$00 per litre. Unleaded is also available, but the majority of rental cars still lack catalytic converters.

Funchal

With a population of 122,000, Funchal is not only the archipelago's largest city but also the undisputed centre of social and cultural life. Administration buildings, the governmental seat, hotels, businesses, shops, and the island's largest port are all located here. The old town is well kept. The large hotels are found on the west coast. All over the city, buildings are being constructed, expanded, and modernised. Funchal is situated on the climatically favourable southern coast and extends into the nearby hills.

Funchal / **History**

Funchal was named after the plant that grew everywhere around the bay at the time of Zarco's and Vaz Teixeira's first landing: o funcho, that is, fennel. The first thing the settlers did was to raze the forest to provided space for houses and farms. The bay at Funchal was thus brought under cultivation. Zarco chose Funchal as his main place of residence, but first lived in Câmara de Lobos for four years until the surrounding land had been made arable — this, the region which was later to become Funchal. Along with Câmara de Lobos, Funchal is on of the oldest settlements in the old Capitania Zarcos *(→History)*, and developed rapidly into the island's largest and most important city. Machico's economic and political significance as "capital" of the Capitania of Tristão Vaz Teixeira never reached Funchal's level of importance. In 1508, Funchal was raised to the status of a city. The entire spectrum of economic and social life took place in Zarco's city. Since its beginnings in the mid 19th century on Madeira, tourism has always concentrated around Funchal. For the pirates, who terrorised the world's seas for many years, Funchal was, of course, also "worth the trip." Funchal did not merely enjoy the benefits of being a wealthy commercial centre, but also suffered the consequences. After the terrible attack of the French pirate Bertrand de Montluc (who plundered and pillaged his way across the island for 15 days) concentrating on Funchal, the three forts were built or fortified further in the hopes that these could defend the city against further onslaughts from the sea *(→Funchal/ Sights)*. The history of Funchal is, for the most part, identical to the history of the island since most historically significant events took place in Funchal *(→History)*. Funchal remains the heart of the archipelago; all administrative and political bodies are located here. The harbour at Funchal is a port for cruise ships, freighters, yachts, and the ferries to Porto Santo. As indicated earlier, Funchal and its "zona hoteleira" is also the centre of tourism.

→Tourism, History .

Funchal / **Quintas, Gardens, and Parks**

The *Quinta do Palheiro Ferreiro* or *Blandy's Garden* is an especially idyllic garden with a delightful atmosphere. The quinta can be reached by taxi or car, or in about 30 minutes with bus no. 29 toward Camacha. Visitor's hours are limited to Monday to Friday from 9:30 am 12:30 pm, since the Blandy family still lives on the grounds. As one might guess from the name, the Blandy family is English and have lived on Madeira since 1811 as vintners and bankers. One of the Madeira wines bears the family name.

Compensation for the rather high admission fee of 450$00 (a portion of which is used to help maintain the Santa Clara convent) comes right at the beginning of a stroll around the gardens: one is confronted with the magnificent blossoms of the camelias. At the height of blossoming between November and April, the camelia hedges are virtually covered with blossoms. Calla lilies, agapanthus, and belladonna lilies thrive. In the front portions of the garden are flower beds filled with very unusual plants, such as the Australian grass tree — the name is befitting when one sees its appearance. A baroque chapel stands on a large lawn, and a bit farther is the old residence. The huge, old laurel trees, oaks, araucarias, and eucalyptus emphasise the lordly flair of this quinta. In the lower portion of the quinta, a tourist centre is presently being built and will include Madeira's second golf course. The *botanical garden* is located somewhat above Funchal and is easily reached by bus (no. 30) or taxi. In the gardens of the former *Quinta de Bom Sucesso* the plants are arranged systematically according to taxonomical classification or geographic origin. Maps of the garden are available at the entrance. Just to the right behind the quinta, which houses the *Natural History Museum,* one finds those species of plants which are indigenous only to Madeira: the endemics *(→ Vegetation).*

The upper garden has a wild, romantic atmosphere and is thick with palms and other trees. Countless lizards scuttle along the paths lined with agapanthus and lilies.

The zone "tropicais" with the tropical plants is especially interesting. These are predominantly plants used in agriculture, whose fruits can also be found at the marketplaces *(→ Fruits).* Worth noting is the *Macadamia planifolia,* crem de la crem among nuts: extremely tasty, but hard to crack.

Anthurias and orchids are cultivated in the greenhouses, and on several terraces one will find an impressive collection of succulents, that is the cactuses and related species.

The *Natural History Museum* is quite small. Nonetheless it does contain some rarities. Here, one will see a multitude of drawers and cabinets which contain an extensive herbarium as well as the fossil collection that helps recount the geologic history of the island. Characteristic sea life and numerous birds are also part of the collection. Open daily from 8 am to 6 pm.

After the botanic garden, one can visit the bird park *Loiros* directly adjacent. The park was opened just two years ago by a Swedish collector and breeder, and a free-flight hall is now being added. The bird park is home to all types of large and small parrots, cockatoos, and budgerigars, among others. One of the owner's goals is to breed endangered species as a contribution to their preservation. Admission is 300$00 for adults and 150$00 for children from 6 to 14 years of age. The park is open daily from 8 am to 6 pm.

Funchal / **Museums**

Almost all of the island's museums are in Funchal, with the exception of the whaling museum in Caniçal *(→ Caniçal)* and the Columbus Museum in Vila Baleira *(→ Porto Santo).*

Instituto de Bordado, Tapeçaria e Artesanato da Madeira:

The enormous tapestry in the spacious marble foyer is certainly impressive with its seven million embroidery stitches (as noted on the sign). The museum is on the second floor. The manufacture of typically Madeiran embroidery is described here, and some especially attractive works are on display.

Other crafts are documented as well, for instance, the weaving of colourful cloth for traditional costumes and basket weaving *(→Baskets)*. The quality is controlled by the "Instituto do Bordado, Tapeçaria e Artesanato" (Institute of Embroidery, Tapestries, and Crafts), which attaches a quality seal and small metal tags that guarantee authentic Madeiran handiwork. One should look for these when purchasing embroidered work in souvenir shops.

Rua Visconde do Anadia 44; open Monday to Friday from 9:30 am to noon and 2 to 5 pm; admission is free of charge.

Paláçio de São Pedro, Museu Municipal:

This natural history museum is a must for those who are interested in the animal life on the island. At the aquarium, one will see specimens of ocean species typical for the archipelago (and for the menus on the island). For instance, there are fanged and black morays, huge groupers, and comical dragon's heads. On the second floor is an esteemed library, and on the third, the collection of taxidermically prepared animals. Birds, insects, fish and marine mammals, including the legally protected monk seal are on display. A relief map provides an overview of the island's geography.

Address: Rua da Mouraria; open Tuesday to Friday from 9 am to 8 pm, Saturday and Sunday from noon to 6 pm; admission is 65$00.

Museu da Cidade:

The City Museum recounts the history of the city and Madeira. From the fennel plant for which the city was named and the city's coat-of-arms to maps of expeditions, trade treaties and town charters, everything is attractively displayed and explained in detail.

Address: Praça do Município; open Monday to Friday 9 am to 12:30 pm and 2 to 5 pm, admission is free of charge.

Museu Photographia Vicentes:

The photography museum reveals another facet of the more recent history of Funchal and Madeira. The family tradition of photography was begun around 1846 by the artistically gifted Vicente Gomes da Silva when photography was still in its infancy, a tradition which was carried on until 1972 by his sons and grandsons. The works document the land and its people as well as famous visitors. A reconstructed old-fashioned photo studio and a handsome collection of old cameras and equipment complete the museum. One can top off a visit to the museum in style at the patio café.

Address: Rua da Carreira 43; open Monday to Friday from 2 to 6 pm; admission is 50$00.

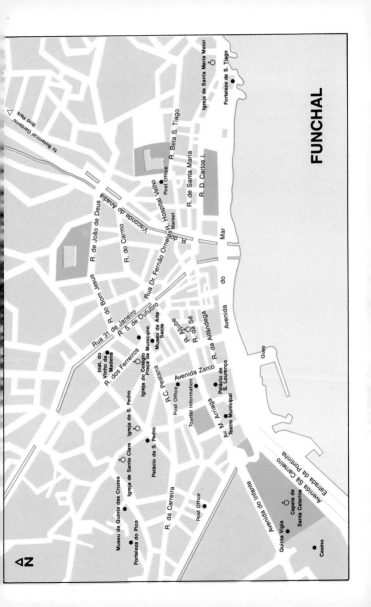

FUNCHAL

△N

to Botanical Gardens/
Bird Park ▽

Igreja de Santa Maria Maior

○ Fortaleza de S. Tiago

R. Bela S. Tiago

Post Office

R. de Santa Maria

R. D. Carlos I.

Visconde do Anadia

R. do Carmo

R. de João de Deus

Rua Dr. Fernão Ornelas

R. Hospital Velho

Top Market

Rua 31 de Janeiro

R. do Bom Jesus

R. S. de Outubro

Inst. do
Vinho da
Madeira ●

R. dos Ferreiros

Praça de
Igreja do Colégio Municipio
● Museu de Arte
Sacra

Albuq.

R. da Sé
○ R. da Sé

Mar

Avenida

do

Mar

● Palácio de S. Pedro

Igreja de S. Pedro ○

Igreja de Santa Clara ○

Museu da Quinta das Cruzes ●

Fortaleza do Pico ●

R. da Carreira

Post Office ●

R.C. Pestana

Post Office ●
Avenida Zarco

Tourist Information ●

Av. Arriaga

R. da Alfândega

Palácio de
S. Lourenço ●

Teatro Municipal ●

Quay

Avenida do Infante

Quinta Vigia ●
○ Capela de
Santa Catarina

Casino ●

Av. Sá Carneiro

Estrada da Pontinha

Museu Quinta da Cruzes:

In the quinta's park are over 50 archaeological stone artifacts, memorials, gravestones and shields, nearly all of which are made of hard Madeiran basalt or marble. The crowning pieces of the collection are definitely the Manueline window frames from an old hospital built in 1507 by King Manuel, after whom this architectural style is named.

At the rear of the park, one finds an expansive orchid cultivation facility that will make any orchid lover's heart beat faster.

In the house itself, art and everyday objects bear witness to the influence of many eras and lands. The furniture was made from sugar crates that were often of Brazilian wood, then decorated with Madeiran wood.

Recovering treasure from a sunken Dutch galleon is also documented. The ship was on its way to East India in 1724 when a storm drove it off course and onto the cliffs off the north coast of Porto Santo where it sank. A great deal of silver and other valuables was recovered, some of which is on display here.

Address: Calçada do Pico 1; open Tuesday to Sunday from 10 am to 12:30 pm and 2 to 6 pm; admission is 100$00.

Museu de Arte Sacra:

In the mid 15th century, trading began between Flanders and Madeira. Sugar was exported in exchange for Flemish paintings. Thus, many of the works originate in 15th century Flanders. Sculptures, silver, and magnificent garments of the finest material illustrate the European influence of the 16th to 18th centuries.

Address: Rua do Bispo 21; open Tuesday to Saturday from 10 am to 12:30 pm and 2:30 to 5:30 pm; admission is 100$00.

Casa Museu Frederico de Freitas:

Frederico Freitas was a Funchal lawyer and collected the highest quality furniture and works of art from the 18th century in his residence. The house's original furnishings and interiors have been maintained as best as possible.

On the ground floor are temporary exhibits that always cover Madeiran or Portuguese themes.

Address: Calçada de Santa Clara; open Tuesday to Sunday from 10 am to 12:30 pm and 2 to 6:30 pm; admission is 100$00 (school children and students free of charge).

Museu Mário Barbeito de Vasconcelos:

This museum, like the Museu Frederico de Freitas, is based on a private collection. The founder of the Barbeito Wine Association collected everything having to do with Christopher Columbus or the history of Madeira, and thus this comprehensive collection came into being, including Columbus portraits from all epochs, sailing maps and model ships.

Along with a visit to the museum, one can use the opportunity to taste the wine at Barbeito Winery's "Diogos Shop."

Address: Avenida Arriaga 48; open Monday to Friday from 9 am to 12:30 pm and 2 to 7 pm; admission is 200$00.

Museu Henrique e Francisco Franco:
The brothers Henrique and Francisco Franco were artistically occupied on Madeira at the beginning of this century. Francisco created the Zarco monument on the Avenida Arriaga, the Sowing Farmer in the Quinta Vigia, and several other sculptures. Other works of art are displayed in this museum. (Because it was renovated in 1991, a more exact description cannot be given.)
Address: Rua João de Deus 13.

Museu de História Natural →*Funchal/Quintas, Botanic Garden*

Funchal / **Sights**

Many streets and buildings in the capital city are reminders of the island's glorious past. For a walking tour of town, one needs a city map (available free of charge at Turismo, including points of interest) and enough time since strolling through heavy traffic and crowded streets can otherwise be somewhat tiring. In any case, one can take advantage of museums visits and shopping trips to discover the historical sites as well.

In the heart of the city lies the largest cathedral, the *Sé,* for which Dom Manuel gave the order to build in 1493, bringing the architect Pêro Enes to Madeira. In the *Museu da Cidade,* there are still documents and sketches made by this master architect, who also erected regal edifices on the mainland. He also designed the old customs building. At the end of the 15th century, Funchal's population had outgrown its former church, Nossa Senhora da Conceiçao, and on what was once the Largo do Duque, houses were torn down to make room for a construction as immense as the cathedral. It was dedicated on the 12th of June 1514. Dom Manuel donated the baptismal font, the pulpit, and various golden jewellry and decorations including the splendid golden processional crucifix now found in the *Museu de Art Sacra.* This building is exemplary of the Manueline style, especially the rear facade with its reddish volcanic stone buttresses and merlons. Named after the regent of the period, this style is characteristic of Portugal's transition into the Renaissance; much more magnificent examples than on Madeira are found on the Portuguese mainland. The cathedral's interior has impressive wooden altar pieces as well as a choir, but most impressive of all is the cedar ceiling with ivory inlays, depicting geometric forms, evidence of the Spanish-Moorish influence. The Baroque age has left its traces here as well, evidenced by various examples.

Mass is held every morning, after which one can look around the cathedral. In addition, it is open to visitors during the weekend in the daytime as well as the evening.

On the Avenida do Mar, two blocks below the Sé, one will find the *Customs House.* This was built in 1477, partly destroyed in the earthquake of 1748 and consequently rebuilt and renovated. Also located on the Avenida do Mar is the *Fortaleza de São Lourenço,* built in 1513 to defend the harbour of Funchal. It is quite flat and has embattlements still armed with cannons aimed seaward. Apparently, the fortress was not as effective as had been hoped: large-scale fortifications were added some time after the pirate attack of 1566. Subsequent rulers and epochs all left their mark on the fort's interior and exterior; today, it is the seat of the civil governor. The most colourful and lively attraction is the *Mercado dos Lavradores* on the city's east side *(→Markets).* The narrow alleyways surrounding the market are dominated by a vibrant chaos of trucks, merchants' stands, and countless pedestrians. Below the market building are the Rua de Santa Maria and the Rua Don Carlos I. The city's oldest houses can be found here, with an atmosphere to match thanks to the numerous restaurants and artisan's shops. Toward the east (leaving town), one comes across the *Capela de Corpo Santo,* and a few metres farther along, one sees the *Forte São Tiago* and the *Santa Maria Maior Church.* The fort was built in 1614 to protect the bay's east flank, and was altered several times during the 18th century. It is still a military facility but it will be vacated and renovated in a few years for the planned military museum. From here, a stairway leads down to a small pebble beach where one can sunbathe and swim right next to fishing boats.

Situated on the climatically favourable southern side of the island, Funchal is without question the most important city of Madeira

There is a nice view of Funchal and the east edge of the bay from Santa Maria do Maior. Its other name, *Igreja do Socorro,* was given to the church in commemoration of the end of an epidemic ("Church of Rescue"); this event is celebrated with a procession every year in May. The way back to the centre of town is down the streets of the old district to Avenida do Mar and the harbour promenade. At the *Marinha,* or yacht harbour, one can find restaurants and bars in every price range. The graffiti on the inside of the outer quay wall is entertaining, and is evidence that Funchal is a port for yachts from all over the world. The star among the harbour locals is probably the "Beatles Boat," whose days at sea are now over since it has been made into a restaurant.

The entire harbour complex is sheltered from the open sea by a long mole, the *Molhe da Pontinha.* This long breakwater connects two small rocky islands (upon which fortresses were once located) with the main island. Large freighters anchor in the modern, industrial harbour and fishing boats bring in their catch of tuna and espada here, to have them inspected by the state fisheries officials before selling them at the market.

But back to the centre of town: going up the Avenida Zarco to the intersection with Avenida Arriaga, one is met by the gaze of a statue of the discoverer, João

On the Praça do Município, the town square, is the very interesting Igreja do Colégio

Gonçalves Zarco. The banks, tourist information, Madeira Wine Company, and city garden Dona Amélia are located on this street running parallel to Avenida do Mar. Across the way, one sees the chamber of commerce with azulejos pictures depicting typical Madeiran scenes and the *Teatro Municipal,* opened in 1888, a stage for plays, concerts, and films. At the end of the block, a street leads down to the "Casa do Turista," where every possible souvenir, local speciality, and handicraft can be purchased in an exquisite and genuine atmosphere at prices to match.

Going up from the Zarco monument along the Avenida Zarco, one passes the *main post office* and *Palácio do Governo Regional* (palace of regional government). At the intersection of Rua da Carreira, Rua das Pretas, and Rua Pestana one turns right to reach the *Praça Municipal,* which is an fine example of the artistic plaster work found in the city. The church *Igreja do Colégio* is located on the north side of this square; to the east, the *Câmara Municipal* (court house); and to the south, the square is bordered by the former episcopal palace, which now houses the Museum of Sacred Art *(→Museums).* The Collegium church was built by Jesuits in the 17th century and is completely Baroque. The court house also contains the *Museu da Cidade,* where one of the island's most unusual means of transportation is displayed in the entrance hall: a sled on metal runners that was pulled across the pavement by oxen.

Northwest of the city's centre are further points of interest accessible via the Rua das Pretas. Here, one will find the *Igreja de São Pedro* and the *Palácio de São Pedro,* which houses the Museu Municipal, founded in 1933. The palace was built during the second half of the 18th century.

The Calçada Santa Clara leads up to the *Convento de Santa Clara* and its church. The convent's inner courtyard and the church may only be visited before and after mass. Both are lovely; the courtyard is graced with Gothic arches. Very old Azulejos (16th to 17th century) have been preserved in the church, and the wooden ceiling demonstrates a clear Moorish influence. Several alterations were made in the 18th century, resulting in an eclectic mixture of artistic and architectural styles. Farther up on the Calçada is the *Quinta da Cruz (→Funchal/Museums).* Just before reaching the quinta, one will come upon an overlook on the left. From here, there is a nice view of the city and western hotel district.

The extension of Calçada Santa Clara is called Calçada do Pico, leading to the *Fortaleza do Pico.* It is not open to the public because the marines use it as a service facility. The first phase of construction on this bulwark was ended in 1632, and the unrestricted view of the bay allowed for timely warnings in the event of pirate attacks.

There are several monuments at the western end of town on the way to the hotel district. The *Monument to the Infant Don Henrique* can be seen from the traffic circle at the end of Avenida Arriaga. Here too, is one entrance to the park at Quinta Vigia, where Francesco Franco's sculpture of the Sowing Farmer stands. Empress Elizabeth of Austria recuperated at the quinta during her illness, and several aristocrats spent their holidays here. At present, the quinta is the seat of government on Madeira. The office where one can book state-run lodgings in the mountains is also located at the quinta (→*Accommodation/Casas do Abrigo*). On the way up to the quinta from the Avenida do Mar is the monument to the Madeiran worker. Very realistically, it depicts the work in the mountains which was necessary to build roads and levadas. The *Capela de Santa Catarina* in the park is one of the oldest churches on the island, commissioned by Dona Constança de Almeida (João Gonçalves Zarco's wife) for the island's first settlers. The interior is early Manueline, and extensive changes were made in the Baroque so that not much remains of the original chapel. Somewhat hidden on the right side of the Avenida do Infante is the building and park of the *Hospício da Princesa D. Amélia,* one of the first lung sanatoria on Madeira.

Numerous hotels line the Avenida do Infante farther along. The round form of the casino stands out; its architect, Oskar Niemeyer, apparently was not interested in a style suited to the landscape and culture.

Much more pleasing to the eye is Reid's Hotel. Its picturesque location is unfortunately somewhat marred by several large, formless hotel blocks around it.

While strolling through the city, one will notice scattered fountains and sculptures, some of which were created by young Madeiran artists, for instance, the monument "Paz e Libertade" at the intersection of Estrada Monumental and Rua do Dr. Pita.

Also a must are the quintas, gardens, and museums (→*quintas, gardens, and museums*).

Funchal / **Practical Information**

Accommodation: The Turismo office will be glad to make arrangements for accommodations. This service is free of charge. The following is just a sample of guest houses and hotels in the centre of Funchal. Prices ranges quoted are for double rooms.

3000$00 to around *4000$00:*

Pensão "Astória," 5th floor, R. João Gago 10, Tel: 2 38 20. English spoken, simple, clean, well maintained, very centrally located behind the Sé Cathedral, two rooms share a bath.

Pensão "Universal," 2nd floor, R. João Tavira, Tel: 2 06 18. Only Portuguese is spoken, very simple, very central.

Residencial "Colombo," R. da Carreira 182, Tel: 2 52 31, 2 52 32. English spoken.

Pensão "Mira-Sol," R. Bela de São Tiago 67, Tel: 2 90 69. English and French spoken, clean, nice atmosphere, well maintained, about 5 minutes from the centre of the city.

4000$00 to around *7000$00:*
Residencial "Monte Rosa," R. João Tavira 31, Tel: 2 90 91. English and French spoken, very centrally located, reservations recommended.
Hotel "Santa Maria," R. Jão de Deus 26, Tel: 2 52 71/2/3. About 5 minutes from the centre of town, swimming pool.

Banks: In the centre of town, the banks are on the Avenida Arriaga. "Montepio Geral" bank lies somewhat hidden at Rua da Sé 16/18: their exchange charge for traveller's cheques is quite reasonable. Even at the Turismo office, the exchange fees are not exceptionally high *(→Tourist Information).*

Bookstores *→Bookstores*

Car Rental *→Car Rental*

Medical Care: District hospital, near the Carlton Hotel, Avenida Luis da Camões, Tel: 4 21 11. A doctor is also on call at this number. Private clinics: Clínica Sta. Catarina, Rua 5 de Outobro, Tel: 2 01 27 and Centro Médico da Sé, Rua do Murças 42, Tel: 3 01 27.

Night Life
The larger hotels all offer evening entertainment and some have discos that are open to non-guests for a cover charge. The casino in the striking round building on the Avenida do Infante is open Monday to Friday from 8 pm to 3 am, Saturday and Sunday from 3 pm to 3 am and the slot machine salon already opens at noon. For dancing, there is the "Vespas Discoteca," Av. Francisco S. Carneiro (predominantly young, Portuguese clientele), in the "Madeira Jazz Club," Travessa Torres 30, and at "Discoteca Reflex," Travessa Praça 3.

Post Office: Avenida Zarco, open Monday to Friday from 8:30 am to 8 pm. Phone booths are open from 8:30 am to 10 pm, Saturdays from 9 am to 12:30 pm. The new main post office is located on Rua Dr. João Brito Câmara, open from 9 am to 6 pm. In the "Zona Hoteleira" is another small post office on Estrada Monumental near the "Lido," and yet another on Rua Conselheiro A. Pestana (behind the marketplace).

Restaurants: Funchal has an abundance of restaurants. The following lists several restaurants that stand out from the crowd owing to their individual style:
Nestled in the cliffs overlooking the ocean is a good (but not necessarily economically priced) seafood restaurant, "Doca do Cavacas," Tel: 76 20 57. From the Estrada Monumental, follow the small pathway between the hotels Madeira Palácio and Duas Torres down to the beach. Reservations are recommended. At first glance, the "Jaquet" restaurant looks like a dimly lit hole-in-the-wall located on the Rua Santa Maria (eastern old town), which isn't very reassuring, especially in the dark; but looking more closely, one will find perhaps the best seafood restaurant in the city. The rickety wooden furnishings stand in sharp contrast to the fresh and excellent food — and to the prices. Even here good food costs good money. The chips (fries) are a minor sensation when the cook seasons the piping hot potatoes with oregano and a generous amount of garlic.

Chinese food can be had at the "Hong Kong Restaurant" at the Olimpo Shopping Centre, Avenida do Infante, Tel: 28 181, and Belgian cuisine is on the menu at the very tiny "Francine's" (also at Olimpo Shopping Centre). At the "Casa dos Reis" at Rua Imperatriz D. Amélia 101, one can order Franco-Portuguese meals. The "Carochinha" at Rua S. Francisco 2-A, Tel: 2 36 95, serves English dishes in addition to coffee and tea at tea time. With Portuguese fado music played in the background, one can dine at "Marcelino's," Travessa da Torre 22-A, Tel: 3 08 34. The "Caravela" restaurant at Avenida do Mar 15 is on the fourth floor from which there is an excellent view of the harbour and ocean. Take-away meals can be ordered at "A Faca" at Avenida do Colégio Militar 6-8, Tel: 6 24 88 and at "A Carreirinha," Rua da Carreira 77, Tel: 2 36 22. On Rua da Queimada de Baixo and Rua da Carreira there are several other restaurants that offer Portuguese and international cuisine at reasonable prices.

Shopping: The best buys on fresh fruit and vegetables can be found at the marketplace. For appropriate times →*Markets*. The largest, least expensive supermarket with the biggest selection is the "Hipermercado Lidosol," open daily from 9 am to 11 pm. Another supermarket with long hours is at the "Shopping Centre Infante," Avenida do Infante, open daily from 10 am to 10 pm. The Rua dos

One example of the diverse landscapes along the Madeiran coast

Tanoeiros is the traditional "shoe street" in Funchal and has a large selection. The Rua de Dr. Fernão Ornelas, Rua das Pretas, and Rua Aljube are Funchal's "shopping streets." The department store "Bazar do Povo" at Rua do Bettencourt 1/5 is still beautifully fitted with old wooden display cases and cabinets and has a truly special flair.

Transportation: The orange municipal buses are ideal for short trips inside the city, for commuting between the hotel zone and the centre, and for shorter excursions — for instance, to Monte, the botanic gardens, or the bird park. Bus routes are posted at the Turismo office and at most bus stops. The buses run often and regularly between 6 am and 11 pm or midnight. It is best to buy tickets ahead of time at the little green kiosks on Avenida do Mar above the yacht harbour or at the bus station.

Tickets for 5 or 10 trips in three different transportation zones or a booklet for one week of travel are available. Both are much less expensive than buying a ticket on the bus. One trip from the 5-ticket package costs 68$00, 103$00, or 137$00, depending on the zone, and a week's ticket costs 2500$00. Bought on the bus, a ticket costs 170$00 per trip.

A historical means of transportation are the basket-sleds from Monte to Funchal (→Monte).

Geography

The Madeira archipelago, which includes Madeira, Porto Santo, the three Desertas and the Selvagens, is a part of the mid-Atlantic island cluster that lies far off the coast of Portugal and Africa between 15° and 14° north latitude and 15° and 30° west longitude. The Azores, which also belong to Portugal, lie slightly north of Lisbon's latitude and about 1,500 km (900 miles) west of the Portuguese capital. 1,000 km (600 miles) to the southeast lies Madeira, also 1,000 km from Lisbon and 600 km (360 miles) from the African continent (same latitude as Casablanca). About 500 km (300 miles) to the south are Spain's Canary Islands, and still farther south, the Cape Verde Islands form the end of the mid-Atlantic island chain. From east to west, Madeira is 57 km (34 miles) long and from north to south 23 km (around 14 miles) at the widest point. The 740 square km (444 square miles) island has a population of 270,000, most of which live in Funchal (122,000) and on the southern coast.

The island's topography is varied and extremely rugged. The highest peaks are slightly east of the island's centre: Pico Ruivo (1,861 metres/6,085 feet), Pico das Torres (1,851 metres/6,053 feet), Pico das Arieiro (1,818 metres/5,945 feet), Pico do Gato (1,790 metres/5,853 feet), and several in the 1,500-metre range (around 4,900 feet). The western regions are dominated by the high plain, Paúl da Serra, which extends as far as the eye can see at an elevation of 1,400 metres (4,580 feet). The sources of most of the rivers is here and around the "picos"; the rivers then flow to the coastal regions through steep, deep valleys and canyons. Terraces were constructed to make farming possible in this rugged terrain and have since become an integral part of the landscape.

The coast consists primarily of lofty cliffs, and only at the mouth of some rivers is it somewhat flatter with a basalt and gravel beach. The second highest coastal cliff in the world is located here: the Cabo Girão plunges 580 metres (1,897 feet) straight down to the sea.

The three Desertas islands ("the deserts") can be regarded as an extension of the southeastern peninsula Ponta de São Lourenço; the Desertas are separated from the main island only by 19 km (11½ miles) of shallow water. The closest Deserta to Madeira is small and flat, almost like a plateau: the Ilhéu Chão. The middle island, Deserta Grande or "big desert," reaches an elevation of 440 metres (264 feet). The third and last island, Bugio, has a slightly rougher outline. These islands, like the Selvagens 280 km (168 miles) to the south, are uninhabited since they support only sparse vegetation, have no drinking water, and do not appear very inviting.

Porto Santo is separated from Madeira by a much deeper trench (2,345 m/7,668 feet). Porto Santo lies 42 km (25 miles) northeast of the "mother island" and has quite a distinct character. It is not as densely populated with only 5,000 residents. The highest point on the 42-square-kilometre island (25 miles) is Pico do Facho, 561 metres (1,834 feet) in altitude. The topography of Porto Santo is on the whole, less extreme than that of Madeira. The northern coast is very steep but not as high, and on the southern coast, the beach at Porto Santo's capital is quite extensive.

Geology

Like many mid-Atlantic islands, the Madeira archipelago is volcanic, possibly formed by the process of the continental drift. In contrast to the Azores, volcanic activity ended here in the last ice age. Geologically speaking, the island is quite young, formed during the Tertiary Period. It is nearly impossible to determine exactly when the first eruptions occurred. The birth of the archipelago was a complex process of many consecutive eruptions and drifting land masses. Thus, one finds many different and alternating layers of rock with impressive colouration. Brick-red lava flows alternate with ochre-yellow layers of volcanic sediments, all of which are punctuated by dark, vertical lava chimneys. This is best seen on the coast at Ponta de São Lourenço, on a hike in the mountains, or on any of the exposed coastal cliffs of Madeira, Porto Santo, and the Desertas. Limestone deposits encased in lava are a geological oddity found above São Vicente at 360 metres (1,177 feet). These marine deposits must have been thrust up with an eruption — an illustration of the tremendous forces involved in the formation of Madeira. A critical factor in ongoing geologic processes is erosion. Wind, rain, the sea, and rivers all erode the rock. Soft volcanic sediments and loose ash deposits erode quickly; with basalt the process is longer. The northern coast is pounded by the wind and waves much more so than the southern coast; thus, it is more rugged and steeper. Rivers in the north drop more sharply than those in the south and thus have enormous erosive force. Frequently, one comes across waterfalls that plunge directly into the ocean or onto a coastal road.

One theory attributes the formation of the Paúl da Serra to erosion, but this is disputable. Similarly, no one can seem to agree on how the Curral das Freiras or the valley of Serra de Água were formed. These basins could either be seen as erosional valleys or old craters. Undisputed is, however, their striking beauty when seen from one of the many overlooks.

On Porto Santo it is impossible to overlook the traces erosion has left in the softer sandstone. This island has less of the hard basalt materials than Madeira, which could in part account for its flatness. Here, too, the northern coast catches the brunt of the wind: ochre-yellow and rust-red cliffs are exposed. Perhaps this island was once much larger; today, one sees the outlying rocky islets, such as Ilhéu de Baixo, de Ferro, das Cenouras and Ilhéu de Cima with the lighthouse, which could once have been connected to Porto Santo.

The form of Madeira and the scattered islands off its coast are evidence of this archipelago's volcanic origins

Hiking

Madeira is truly a hiker's paradise. The island's most beautiful areas are best discovered on long walks. Even though the terrain is mountainous and dissected by deep valleys, it is possible to walk long distances along the levadas without noticeable climbs. Some of these paths are wide, easy, and safe, while others are very narrow, exposed, and at dizzying heights. For any hike, one needs good directions, and sometimes it's better to have a guidebook, a map, and the following equipment: sturdy, non-slip shoes or boots, a raincoat, light clothing, and in summer a hat and sunscreen in addition to the mandatory warm clothing (e.g. sweater and long trousers). One should also bring a compass, pocket lamp, enough food, plenty of water or tea, and a bus schedule for Madeira. If planning a hike on one's own, one must bear in mind that the routes take much more time than is given in the guidebooks, since breaks are not included in the hiking times. It is important to know if and when a bus operates back to the hotel, or if one should order a taxi. Twilight is very short here, and one should not hike in the dark. The weather is changeable and often quite different on the north than on the south side (→Climate). After a heavy rain, some paths are not passable, and rain is especially frequent in spring, making many trails muddy or flooding them. This is hardly

A hike from Santo de Serra to Camacha leads through an especially beautiful landscape

a problem in summer. A pocket lamp is needed for those levada hikes which include tunnels. If a hiking guidebook mentions the importance of having no fear of heights for a particular route, this should by all means be taken seriously and one should avoid overestimating one's own abilities. In the worst case, turning back or walking in the levada itself (in the water) is recommended if the path alongside the levada looks too unsafe or steep.

The following describes only a few of the trails on which one can discover the island's beautiful diversity. They lead through various regions with differing degrees of difficulty.

The Peaks Tour / **Pico do Arieiro, Pico Ruivo**

On this hike, one experiences Madeira's beautiful mountain world and if the weather is clear, there is an unparalleled view. The trailhead at Pico do Arieiro is accessible by car. Unfortunately, bus no. 103 runs only as far as Poiso, from where one must take a taxi the rest of the way. The trail is about 8 km long (around 5 miles) and is quite strenuous. It is not always secured but is well maintained, and takes about five hours for the hike.

Starting from Pico do Arieiro, one follows the sign toward Pico Ruivo, first down a number of steps and later along the wide, paved path. After 15 minutes, one comes to a *Miradouro* (viewpoint), and after 30 minutes to a nice picnic site. The first tunnel (after about one hour of hiking) is 100 metres (327 feet) long and goes under the Pico do Gato. The trail winds along the rocks, which have a mottled appearance due to the plate-sized aeoniums and multicoloured lichens growing on them. There is one more long tunnel (150 metres, 491 feet) and two shorter ones (about 20 metres or 65 feet). One passes through the last one after about an hour and 40 minutes; a sign points the way after that. The hanging orange lichens on gnarled trees are quite striking. Ferns and mosses grow in the damp caves along the trail.

After a strenuous climb along a stepped trail shaded by tree heather, one reaches first the Pousada do Pico do Arieiro and 10 or 15 minutes later, the summit of Pico do Arieiro is attained. From here, there is an outstanding view of Ponta de São Lourenço and the Desertas to the east, of the northern and southern coasts, the mountains, and the high plain, Paúl da Serra. One takes the same trail going back and should save a bit of strength for the stairs leading back up to Pico do Arieiro. Sunrise and sunset are tremendous in the mountains, and the colourful rock faces, clouds, and light combine to put on a spectacular display of nature.

→*Pico do Arieiro, Pico Ruivo*

The Eastern Tip / **Caniçal, Ponta de São Lourenço**

The eastern tip is very different from the rest of the island, which is normally lush in vegetation. This region, however, indicates how it must look on the Desertas.

With bus no. 113 from Funchal, one reaches Caniçal in an hour and a half; the bus also stops in Machico. The whale museum in Caniçal is worth a visit as well (→ *Caniçal*).

At the village square, cross the bridge heading east, bear to the left at the second intersection, and turn right in front of the post office onto the ER 101-3. There is little traffic on this road making it well suited for hiking. After a total of 4 km (2½ miles), one reaches a picnic site with a nice panorama. A few metres farther along is a stairway down to Madeira's legendary "little beach." Continuing along the road, one passes a meadow where a small chapel stands on a hill. After one more kilometre (½ mile), one sees the parking area at *Baía de Abra*. From here, follow the wide gravel road to a path that leads to the right toward the "island's tip." After 15 minutes one comes upon a trail with a spectacular view which should not to be missed.

From this point on, the trail continues uphill and is somewhat rough, narrow, and at times difficult to find. A few white markings are helpful. In another 45 minutes one will reach the *Casa do Sardinha* hill which looks like a small, overgrown oasis. From here, one can go out to land's end and, after a well-earned rest, return via the same route.

If one takes a taxi from Caniçal to Prainha or its parking area, the hike is 5 km (3 miles) shorter. The company of goats or grazing cattle is more amusing than it is dangerous.

Curral das Freiras / **From Corticeiras to Curral das Freiras**

On this hike, one explores the valley that one repeatedly sees ahead and below. One crosses the *Ribeira do Curral* and climbs back up to the village. The hike is strenuous because of the number of climbs and descents along its 10 km (6 miles). Corticeiras is the end of the line for bus no. 96 from Funchal. The trailhead is at the Trafo station somewhat below the bus stop. From here, one goes up along the wide, paved path to the left and comes to the *Quinta Miss Muchacho* about 10 minutes later. From this point, one takes the path uphill to the left again. Next, there is a series of switchbacks uphill along utility roads in the eucalyptus forest. An hour later, one will reach the *Boca dos Namorados* which has a stunning preliminary view of the Curral das Freiras. The narrow trail continues to the left through a lovely pine and eucalyptus forest. Shortly after seeing a telephone pole, one follows the path around a sharp curve to the right and an hour and 40 minutes later, one arrives at the *Pico do Cedro*. After two hours, there is an inviting place to stop in the shade of chestnut trees.

Two hours and 40 minutes into the hike, one crosses the first stream, which is unfortunately also used as a cesspit. A short while later, the paved path leads up to the left past small gardens, up the stairs and down the stairs... crossing several bridges. The valleys and streambeds are beautiful as long as one looks upward; downstream, sadly enough, they are filthy.

After three and a half hours, one comes to the big bridge over the Ribeira do Curral. Gathering one's strength, one starts up the innumerable steps to the village of Curral das Freiras, gaining 200 metres (around 650 feet) in elevation. After crossing the Levada do Curral, one is finally at the top 4 hours and 10 minutes after beginning the hike.

In the village, one can enjoy refreshments at one of the a cafés and wait for bus no. 81 back to Funchal.

Levada dos Piornais / **From Funchal to Vitória**

This walk heads above Funchal's hotel district to the west. Arrival and departure are no problem since many buses are in operation along the ER 215 to Funchal. There are hardly any changes in elevation, but at some spots one must be sure-footed and free from any fear of heights.

The beginning of this hiking trail is on Estrada Monumental. The intersection with Rua Dr. Pita cannot be overlooked, thanks to the trapezoid-shaped island in the middle of the street. One follows the Rua Dr. Pita uphill; on the right is the Quinta Magnólia, with another quinta with a high wall opposite. Behind this quinta, one turns left.

After going a few hundred metres, one takes the first narrow street up to the right. Having reached the top, one sees a green railing with several steps leading to the levada. From here on it will be easy to find the way, and the levada is covered with concrete slabs in some places making the hike even easier. In the first half hour, one is still in the less attractive residential and hotel areas, and one might become dizzy at some points along the steep wall.

After 40 minutes, one must cross a street and bear slightly to the right. The path narrows until reaching the broad concrete slabs once more. The next road is crossed after and hour and 15 minutes or so. From there, one continues on the sloped, paved path. Rounding a left-hand curve, the trail leads upward to the right behind a house; then one walks along the levada again.

Shortly thereafter, one comes to the next road and its highway construction site. It is best to go up the old road to the right, and cross the new road to get back to the levada. The path continues through banana plantations and past residential gardens.

An hour and 40 minutes into the walk, one comes to a paved path and a levada sluice. From here on, only the most sure-footed should continue, since the levada path becomes extremely narrow and ends 10 minutes later — but the view down into the valley of Ribeira dos Socorridos is fantastic. One returns down along the paved path to Vitória. From here, there is a bus back to Funchal. The entire walk takes about 2 hours.

Rabaçal / **Risco Waterfall and the 25 Springs**

Rabaçal is one of Madeira's most idyllic spots, and the best idea is to combine these walks with an excursion to Paúl da Serra to get an impression of the stark contrasts in the island's landscapes. There is no bus connection all the way to Rabaçal; bus no. 107 runs to Canhas and from there one must take a taxi. The same is true for the return trip.

These are pleasant little walks and aside from a few stairs, rarely strenuous. One starts either at the water works or at the inn in Rabaçal. The path is 3.5 km (around 2 miles) long and paved. At the inn, the rustic tables and benches and the fountain surrounded by lush greenery make an inviting setting for a picnic. Starting here, one follows the sign in front of the house which points to the right and reads "25 Fontes, Risco." Go down the wooden steps to the next sign, "25 Fontes" that points to the right. After 10 minutes there is an crossing of paths with a branch off to the left; for the time being, one remains on the upper path. Here along the levada, water always runs down from the mountains, and everything is covered by a thick, soft carpet of moss, lichens and ferns. Light plays among the green branches and sparkles on the water. In only 20 minutes, one has reached the Risco Falls viewpoint, not necessarily without getting wet! From here, one has a sweeping view of the Ribeira da Janela's green valley. Going back to the crossing (about 30 minutes) and following the sign "25 Fontes," one descends slightly to the Levada das 25 Fontes; here one goes to the right. Twenty minutes later a stream crosses the levada flowing through a cement canal, wet feet are to be expected. At this point, it is best to overcome any fear of heights, but one can also hold on to the levada wall, which is about waist high at this point. After an hour and 20 minutes, one comes to a bridge and a levada sluice, and off to the side lies a turquoise-coloured pond with water streaming into it from all sides. From this point, one can either go back to Rabaçal or farther along the lower levada and to Madeira's longest tunnel. This detour takes about 20 minutes.

In all, one should count on spending about two hours to see everything and have time to picnic and rest as well.

Levada da Serra / **From Santo da Serra to Camacha**

This hike is an easy one for people with a bit of endurance; the route is about 14 km (8½ miles) long and follows a gentle course along the levada. To reach Santo da Serra, one can take bus no. 77 through Camacha and no. 20 or 25 through Santa Cruz. This trip can be combined with a visit to the *Quinta do Santo da Serra* (→*Santo da Serra*). To return from Camacha to Funchal, take bus no. 29 or 77 (coming from Santo da Serra).

In Santo da Serra, one must follow the street from the village square to the left past the church to the intersection, where a small blue sign on the right points the way to the levada (2 km/1¼ miles). Somewhat farther (5 minutes), a second sign points diagonally off to the left, and one continues on the gravel path. Gaining a few metres in elevation, one will reach a crossing, where there is a sign for Camacha to the left. The path is wide and pleasant; liverworts, club moss, and ferns grow along the levada. This continues for a while until crossing the ER 202 after about an hour and a half. At the next fork in the path, bear to the right. One hour and 50 minutes into the walk there is a 5 metre long tunnel (around 16 feet) leading into one of the characteristic valleys with a waterfall, terraced fields, and willow trees. One must fords two streams, passing a ramshackle old house. After two hours and 40 minutes, one reaches a crossing with a stone marker pointing the way to *Águas Mansas* to the left, but keep following the trail straight ahead. One will then come to a "levada crossing," and after 3 hours and 15 minutes, the path crosses a road, beyond which the levada is no longer visible.

The gravel road meets up with a paved road leading to Camacha, but the trail goes straight on down a stairway to a smaller road that also leads to Camacha. This walk takes four hours and 20 minutes to reach its destination (→*Camacha*). It is a simple matter to vary this walk, since the path along the Levada da Serra is well-maintained from Ribeiro Frio to Choupana or Monte. Madeirans like to help and will give directions by gesturing if necessary.

Levada dos Tornos / **From Blandy's Garden to Monte**

This walk in the vicinity of Funchal covers several sights at once. It leads through a lovely valley, and one has repeated views of Funchal, the south coast, and the Desertas.

Leaving Funchal early in the morning with bus no. 29 toward Camacha, one can tell the bus driver "Blandy's Garden." The driver will stop on a street from which a path leads down for several minutes to the Quinta Palheiro Ferreiro.

The walk begins back up on the street where the bus stopped. Somewhat above the bus stop one will find the levada. One can also take the prettier route from the quinta's entrance to the right, then after 20 metres (around 65 feet), turn up to the left past some houses and gardens to reach the Levada do Tornos. Here, one turns left and goes upstream, crossing the road after a few hundred metres and continuing parallel to it for a while.

Half an hour later, one will cross another road, after which the levada is covered with cement slabs. After one hour, one will reaches a water house and then a quinta with a trampled path above it leading around the grounds.

After an hour and 40 minutes one will comes to *Romeiros,* a little settlement, passing close by its houses and gardens. One then goes down two steps and follows the paved path that passes by houses and the village store. This route leads to rock stairs that descend into the lovely *Curral dos Romeiros* after about 10 minutes; in another 10 minutes back up to *Babosas.* From here, it is not much farther to

Monte. The path leads past the chapel *Nossa Senhora da Conceição* and the quinta with the same name, until arriving at the church in Monte.

From here, one can go on uphill to *Terreiro da Luta,* but after walking so far already, another steep, 25-minute climb can be quite tiring. To the right next to Monte's church, the road leads up past the bars and souvenir shops.

After visiting the church, though, a sled ride down into Funchal may be more pleasant *(→Monte and Monte/Vicinity).*

Otherwise, one can get back to Funchal with buses no. 20, 21, or 22 from Largo da Fonte.

History

Most history books set the date of the Madeira archipelago's "official" discovery as 1418 or 1419. The island's existence was probably known to the Phoenicians, but this was lost during the course of the centuries. The archipelago is mentioned on maps for the first time in 1339 and 1359 ("Carta de Ducert" and "Atlas Mideceu"). In these works, Madeira is called "Isola de Legname" or wood island, which corresponds to the Portuguese "Ilha da Madeira." The names "Porto Santo" (holy harbour) and "Deserte" for the Desertas (the deserts) also appear. Thus, it is highly likely that Madeira was known to seafarers even before 1418 since Spanish and Portuguese sailing vessels often visited the Canary Islands in the 14th century and Madeira and Porto Santo are easily visible from the sea route to the Canaries.

Several legends have grown up around the discovery and formation of Madeira. There are always those who adamantly maintain that Madeira and the Azores represent the remnants of the legendary city of Atlantis. The following saga is often told in conjunction with stories of Madeira's discovery:

A poor young nobleman, Robert Machim, who lived during Edward III's time (1327-1377), fell in love with a young lady of high social standing, Ana de Arfet, who, for her part, was quite fond of him. Her father, however, absolutely rejected him as a husband for his daughter and saw to it that the two were separated and Robert was even imprisoned. Robert succeeded in freeing himself and with the assistance of friends, fled with Ana to France. Unfortunately, the ship was caught up in a storm and driven onto the shore of an island. The heavily wooded island was uninhabited. The young couple spent a few happy days there. Then, sadly, the ship and its crew abandoned them there — in some accounts, the sailors mutiny; in others, yet another storm drives them out to open sea. Ana was so crushed by this catastrophe that she died of despair and a broken heart shortly thereafter. Robert buried her — and here again the opinions of the storytellers diverge: some say Robert dies of loneliness, longing, and despair; others say he builds a seaworthy vessel, is again swept away by a storm, captured by Moors and imprisoned. It is at this point that he meets his traitorous mates, fights them, arouses the interest of the local caliph, tells his sad story and is set free.

These are just the most impressive versions of the seamen's yarns revolving around Robert Machim and his beloved Ana de Arfet. The Portuguese have, of course, changed Robert's English name to "Robert o Machino," and the bay in which his ship is said to have run aground is even called Machico.

In any case, it is a historical fact that in 1418, the seafarers João Gonçalves Zarco and Tristão Vaz Teixeira rather coincidentally landed at Porto Santo after bad weather forced them off course. Zarco, who wrote his name "Zargo" in a document from 1447, and Vaz Teixeira had been sent by Prince Dom Henrique o Navegador (Henry the Navigator) to explore the coast of Morocco. Dom Henrique (1394-1460) was given the epithet "the Navigator" because of his contributions to sailing and support of expeditions. The island was valued by the Portuguese for its rich forest, fertile soil, and convenient geographic location that predestined it as a station for longer discovery expeditions. Yet another advantage was that the archipelago was uninhabited, which meant future settlers would have no unpleasant confrontations with "unruly natives," as was the case with Spanish settlers and the native people of the Canary Islands. Dom Henrique had the island settled under the direction of the two discoverers and a certain Bartolomeu Perestrelo in 1419. Madeira and Porto Santo were divided into three *Donatarios.* Zarco and Teixeira divided Madeira in half diagonally: roughly, the line ran between Porto Moniz on the northern coast and Caniço on the southern.

João Gonçalves was about 30 years old when he discovered Madeira and Porto Santo. He was a knight of the prince's court and had proven himself in battle against the Moors. He administered the *Capitania* Funchal for over 40 years and presumably died in 1467 at a ripe old age. Because of his high standing with the royal family, he received the epithet *Zargo. Tristão Vaz's* background is unknown, but it was more humble than Zarco's. He established himself as a seafarer and companion of the crown prince. Tristão Vaz married into one of Portugal's most highly regarded families and called himself "Vaz Teixeira" from then on. He died in a small village in Algarve when he was well over 80, after having governed Machico for more than 50 years. *Bartolomeu Perestrelo,* a nobleman of Italian descent, pressured the prince to give him Porto Santo as *Donatario* as his fief for life. Although unfamiliar with the island, he embarked full of hope with Zarco and Vaz Teixeira to colonise the uninhabited archipelago. Perestrelo did not find the living conditions on Porto Santo ideal as they were on Madeira. Water shortages, agriculture that was only possible with extreme hardship, and a plague of rabbits (this was his doing and due to the absence of natural predators, they reproduced out of control and ate the crops) caused him to leave the island after only two years. His third marriage produced a daughter, D. Filipa Perestrelo y Moniz, who went down in history as the wife of Christopher Columbus.

All sorts of legends and stories have evolved concerning the settlement of Madeira as well. They say Madeira burned for seven years straight when the settlers cleared the forest with fire. Of course, this can be interpreted as slash-and-burn clearing that went on for 7 years. It is also said that the first settlers stood in the ocean for two days and nights to save themselves from the fire gone out of control.

For their part, the captains bestowed the land as fiefdoms upon noblemen and merchants who committed themselves to making the land arable within a certain time frame. If they were unable to keep their end of the deal, the land was given to more capable settlers. Fields were cultivated with the "help" of African, Moorish, or Canary Island slaves, prisoners, or free farmers from Portugal.

Agriculture thrived so well that within a short period of time, the island was producing enough to make it self-sufficient and even for export. Grain, wine, lumber, and sugar cane were the most important products. From the beginning, farmers terraced their fields to make the fertile but precipitous slopes suited to planting and harvesting. The water problem — in short, too much in the north and not enough in the south — was solved by building the *levadas,* or water canals (→Levadas). Trade in slavery was also a profitable venture, and had it not been for the unpaid work of forced labourers and slaves, Madeira would not have experienced such an economic boom. In 1858, slavery in Portugal was officially abolished, but during the previous 100 years it had already been drastically reduced.

The greatest profits were to be made with the high-demand commodity of sugar. Thus, sugar was nearly the only crop planted, and as early as the 1560's, grain had to be imported. The discovery and colonisation of Brazil, however, dried up this source of income for Madeira since more sugar cane could be cultivated in Brazil with much less effort (fewer workers, no terracing) than on the steep slopes of this Atlantic island. Settlers on the Azores took advantage of Madeira's sugar-monoculture phase to establish itself as Portugal's chief grain supplier. Around 1530, Madeirans intensified their production of wine, importing grapevines from Cyprus and Crete (→Wine).

The island was rapidly populated; only 100 years after its discovery, about 5,000 people of various nationalities lived on Madeira; they were quick to recognise Madeira's value as a site for businesses and trade station for new and much sought after products from the colonies in the recently discovered New World. Merchants, speculators, and nobility from France, England, Castile, Flanders, and Italy brought in money and ideas, and invested fortunes in sugar cane cultivation and agriculture. Since its discovery in 1418, the Madeira archipelago has been a province of Portugal with the same rights as the mainland; thus, it has never suffered exploitation of raw materials at the hands of the mother country, unlike the overseas colonies. Madeira's history is therefore closely intertwined with that of Portugal. The age of expansionism and the resulting prosperity left its traces on Madeira as well: the Manueline architectural style and a rich tradition of sacred art bearing a strong

Flemish influence were characteristic of the little province in the Atlantic. The "division of the world" between Spain and Portugal (treaties of 1494 and 1529) and the Spanish dominion over Portugal from 1580 to 1640 had their influence on Madeira, yet the political and social effects on the remote Atlantic islands were never as marked as on the mainland. The "real" catastrophes that afflicted the islands were of a different nature: epidemics, famine, earthquakes, and pirate attacks made life difficult for the population. Sea robbers, who always saw the prosperous but vulnerable islands as full of fat booty only too easy to grab, terrorised the oceans well into the 19th century. Both famous and infamous is the attack executed by the French pirate Bertrand de Montluc. Equipped with eleven ships and an estimated 1,300 men, he plundered and burned Madeira for 16 days in1566. Madeira's population made no earnest attempt to defend itself for fear that this would incite even worse reactions on the part of the better-armed fiends.

Porto Santo with its unprotected sandy shores was an easy port for pirates, and the population's only defence was to flee into the mountains of the island's interior. Madeirans and Porto Santans developed a "pirate warning system" which consisted of constantly watching the ocean from lookout points and using smoke signals to inform the neighbouring island as soon as the skull-and-crossbones appeared on the horizon. Madeirans, too, sought to rescue themselves by hiding in the less accessible interior whenever pirates were sighted *(→Curral das Freiras)*. A further milestone in Madeira's history was the marriage of the English King Charles II to Portuguese noblewoman Catarina of Bragança. Portugal's political and social situation was still very unstable after 60 years under Spanish rule (1580-1640). An alliance with Spain's arch-enemy England would enormously improve the military and political position of the weakened Iberian state. Portugal gave Catarina a handsome dowry to take along to England, almost including the "flowering island province Madeira." With this marriage contract, the English received the right to settle on Madeira and extensive trade allowances. Many English merchants immigrated to Madeira as a result and invested in sugar, wine, and slave trading. Madeira, too, profited from the alliance, since only Madeira and port wine were allowed to be shipped directly to the overseas English colonies — all other goods had to first be shipped to England before being transported from there to the colonies. This created a "wine boom" on Madeira, in which English merchants also participated to a great extent since Madeira wine was a favourite all over the British Empire *(→Wine)*. The British quickly integrated into Madeiran society and rose to become the island's social elite. A few British families had a crucial impact on the history and economy of the island, for instance, the Blandys *(→Funchal/Quintas, Gardens, and Parks)* and the Leacocks *(→Wine)*.

During the 18th century, Madeira was hit by two cholera epidemics (1724 and 1765) and shaken by a strong earthquake.

As all of Europe shook with fear of Napoleon, Portugal held on to its alliance with England, and England "occupied" Madeira from 1801 to 1807 to protect it from a possible French invasion. The relations between the "occupying forces" and the population were friendly to warm-hearted. The English left in 1814 after attaining considerable influence on trade. Napoleon himself did finally come to Madeira, that is, on his way into exile in Saint Helena (1815). The ship lay anchored off the coast to restock provisions. The island's reigning governor cordially welcomed Napoleon with a glass of Madeira, but the toppled emperor was not allowed to come ashore.

The year 1860, however, was more important in the island's own history, since it marks the introduction of embroidery by the Englishwoman Elisabeth Phelps. This represented an invaluable source of income for countless families, since (although it was then as now underpaid) commercial embroidery meant employment for women and a highly important export article, as it remains today.

The Madeirans desperately needed an additional source of income in the 19th century; they found themselves in a severe economic crisis due to the decline of sugar exports. From 1851 to 1856 a plant mildew killed most of the grapevines, and in 1873, a grape aphid plague destroyed most of the remaining grapevines. By genetic crossing and planting a much more robust but qualitatively inferior American grape variety, Madeiran viniculture was saved *(→Wine)*.

It was around this time that the cultivation of bananas gained new significance since the development of refrigeration on ships allowed transport and consequently export abroad.

The 19th century was also marked by political unrest and crises. The Portuguese royal family fled Napoleon's troops in 1807 and went to Brazil, to finally return to Lisbon in 1820. The populace began to rebel, but was this was pacified by introducing a constitutional monarchy in 1822 which gave citizens more rights and freedom. Brazil declared its independence, unleashing an economic crisis in the Portuguese motherland because it had no productive industry or agriculture of its own. Domestic unrest, government crises, revolts, and famine were part of everyday Portuguese life. These problems also affected Madeira, as reflected in the people's revolt of 1847. Floods (1813), earthquakes (1815), and a cholera and smallpox epidemic (1858 and 1872) made life even more difficult for the Madeirans. Because of corruption, the death of one monarch after another, a continuing financial crisis, and the decay of the traditional political parties, the constitutional monarchy was replaced by founding the Republic of Portugal on October 5, 1910. Madeira was given extensive administrative autonomy by the mother country. However, the new republic also stood on shaky ground: between 1211 and 1926 there were 44 changes in government. In 1916, Germany declared war on England's ally, Portugal, because it had confiscated German ships in response to pressure from the Allied Forces. On December 3rd and 12th, 1916, German submarines bombarded French ships and English steamers in Funchal's harbour. The city was also hit in the attacks, and several people were killed.

The military staged a coup in 1926, and the Republic of Portugal came to an end. António de Oliveira Salazar became prime minister in 1932 and ruled until 1968 as fascist dictator in his "Estado Novo," or new state. On far-away Madeira, the dictator's influence was by no means as great as on the mainland, especially since the island was not as isolated from the outside world as was the mainland, in spite of geography. Tourism played an important role on Madeira even then. People with lung diseases, rich English tourists, and cruise ship passengers visited the island, brought hard currencies, and influenced the lives of the inhabitants. When Gago Coutinho and Sacadura Cabral landed on the bay of Funchal for the first time with a seaplane on March 22, 1921, it marked the beginning of regular air traffic between England, Funchal, and Lisbon. Air traffic was stopped in 1958 after two crashes, but resumed in 1960 when the airport on Porto Santo was built. In 1921, Emperor Karl I of Austria and Empress Zita went into exile on Madeira. Austria's former emperor died on April 11, 1922 and with the sympathy of a large portion of the population, was buried at the church in →*Monte.* In 1931, a law was passed which gave flour mill owners on Madeira the right to regulate flour imports. This law set off a revolt in the Madeiran populace against Salazar's regime, highly dissatisfied with his "Estado Novo." Although all other important events originated on the mainland, the only public resistance against Salazar during his entire regime began on the island. The "spark of revolution," however, did not set fire on the mainland, and the "hunger revolt" of 1931 was quashed by government troops after three weeks.

The years-long, exhausting, and senseless guerrilla warfare in the colonies of Angola and Mozambique coupled with Portugal's domestic political problems brought on the nearly bloodless "carnation revolution" by the military opposition on April 25, 1974. The Madeirans, too, had great expectations of the new government, which set a socialist course. Numerous reforms, nationalisation, and the restructuring of agriculture into cooperatives (especially in Algarve and Alentejo) met with protest among Madeira's conservative rural population. For the first time in Madeira's 500-year history, a separatist right-wing organisation supporting the independence of the archipelago from Portugal gained strength. Its influence remained limited, however, since its militant activities found little support among the populace. The influence of the socialist government was not as marked on Madeira as on the mainland; large property owners and merchants were not disenfranchised as they were in Portugal itself. Today, the island provinces of Madeira and the Azores are independent to a great extent. They have their own regional government and parliament, their own administration, taxation and tariffs. They send representatives to parliament in Lisbon.

Portugal's membership in the EC (1986) has also brought Madeira many advantages and disadvantages.

→*Economy*

Holidays and Celebrations

National Holidays

New Year's Day, Shrove Tuesday, Good Friday, Anniversary of the 1974 Revolution on April 25, Labour Day on May 1, Feast of Corpus Christi, national holiday on June 10, Assumption on August 15, 1910 Proclamation of the Republic on October 5, All Saints' Day on November 1, 1640 liberation from Spanish rule on December 1, Immaculate Conception on December 8, and Christmas (December 25).

Celebrations

All year long, Madeirans celebrate two basically different kinds of festivals. First, there are the religious celebrations spread out over the church calendar, and secondly, folk festivals and fairs are held, at which natural events such as the harvest are celebrated. In both cases, the population participates enthusiastically, usually with parades, folk dances and songs, and a great variety of culinary specialties. High points of the year include the big festivals in Funchal organised in part by the tourism bureau, for instance, Carnival (Mardi Gras) and the anona, chestnut, apple, flower, and wine festivals. Other important celebrations occur at Easter, Christmas, and New Year's Eve with its lavish display of fireworks.

The *Romarias* have a long tradition. They may be described as church christening or pilgrimage celebrations. Outside Funchal, these are not celebrated as pompously; in the country, there are fewer tourists and the Madeirans celebrate among themselves. In the following, the festivals are listed chronologically.

January: On January 5, the eve of the Feast of the Three Kings, singers disguised as the Kings stroll around in some villages.

On January 15, the Festival of Santo Amaro takes place in Santa Cruz. This marks the end of Christmas festivities.

February: Towards the end of the month or the beginning of March, Carnival is celebrated everywhere, but especially extensively in Funchal. The colourful parade, which culminates at the Praça do Municípo, is just one part of the wild, three-day celebration, modelled after Carnival in Brazil.

March: Just recently, the Anona Festival has started being celebrated in Faial at anona harvest time. *Festa da Anona* is celebrated in Funchal as well, and the luscious fruit is served in a variety of ways everywhere.

April: Easter is an important celebration in every community, and processions and special masses are held during the week before Easter Sunday. In Ribeira Brava, an elaborate Passion Play is performed on Good Friday in front of the church. In mid April, the Flower Festival is celebrated in Funchal, for which incredible quantities of blossoms are used in decorating wagons and streets. On Sunday, there is a parade through town, and the most beautiful bouquets are displayed on Avenida Arriaga. Folklore and music groups contribute to the festivities and a classical concert is given at the Teatro Municipal.

May: Pentecost or Espirito Santo is observed on Madeira, and is especially celebrated in Camacha.

June: The feast of *Santo António* takes place on June 13 in Santo da Serra. On the 24th, the feast of *São João* is celebrated in Funchal, São Martinho, Câmara de Lobos, Lombada do Ponta do Sol and Fajãda Ovelha. *São Pedro* is observed on the 29th in Ribeira Brava and Câmara de Lobos.

Towards the end of the month, sheep shearing is another cause for celebration. The happenings at the *Festa das Tosquias* in Santana and Paúl da Serra are quite lively.

At some point (the date varies), the *Festa da Cereja* or cherry festival takes place.

July: On the 22nd in Madalena do Mar and Porto Moniz, the *Festa da Santa Maria Magdalena* is observed. In the second half of the month, an agricultural exhibition takes place in Porto Moniz, which is naturally accompanied by a sort of county fair. A folklore festival is staged in Santana.

August: On the 14th and 15th, Madeira's patron saint *Nossa Senhora do Monte* is honoured with the island's largest celebration next to Christmas. On this occasion, almost the entire population goes to church in Monte to ask that their prayers be heard. A great procession carries the portrait of the manifestation through decorated streets. Following the procession, the island's largest folk festival is celebrated. On the same day on the neighbouring island of Porto Santo, the festival of *Nossa Senhora da Graça* is observed, which also can be traced back to a legendary manifestation of Mary.

On the last Sunday of the month, the festival of *Nossa Senhora do Livramento* (Our Lady of Salvation) is celebrated in Curral das Freiras.

September: In mid-September, several harvest festivals take place, for instance the *Festa da Vindima* (wine grape harvest) in Funchal and Estreito de Câmara de Lobos. Offering wine tasting and tours, the wineries seek potential customers. The apple harvest is celebrated with, of course, the *Festa da Maçã.*

Another important happening is the *Festa da Nossa Senhora do Faial* on September 8 in Faial. On the same date, a romaria in honour of *Nossa Senhora dos Remédios* takes place in Quinta Grande. In Caniço, the *Festa da Nossa Senhora do Livramento* is celebrated on the second Sunday of the month, and the *Festa da Nossa Senhora da Piedade* (Feast of Our Lady of Mercy) takes place on the third Sunday of the month in Caniçal.

October: On the first Sunday, the feast of *Nossa Senhora do Rosário* is observed in São Vicente. In Machico on the 9th, there is an impressive procession to commemorate the miraculous rescue of a portrait of Christ from the sea *(→Machico).* During the *Festa das Bandas* towards the end of the month, local music groups get together in Ribeira Brava.

November: A lovely autumn festival amid beautiful landscapes takes place in Curral das Freiras: the *Festa da Castanha.* Near the end of the month, the *Santo André Avelino* festival is observed in Canhas' Chapel Carvalhal.

December: Christmas festivities begin early. Music and dance groups perform outdoors, and the traditional Christmas confection "Bolo del Mel" can be found everywhere. Between December 8 and January 6, all of Funchal is aglow with Christmas lights.

Madeira is well known for its magnificent fireworks on New Year's Eve. At hardly another time is the harbour so full of cruise ships and yachts, from which the spectacle can perhaps be best observed.

International Press

English-language newspapers and magazines can be found at hotels and kiosks. There are also several free advertisement papers published in many languages, which also contain information on current events. They can be found at hotels and shops.

Of course, Madeira has its own Portuguese-language newspapers: "Diário de Notícias" and "Jornal da Madeira."

Jardim do Mar

The "garden of the sea" overlooks the ocean. Going along the southwest coast on ER 101 and following the signs toward the coast, Jardim do Mar is reached after 4 km. The road was recently built, as can be seen by its good condition. Jardim do Mar has been accessible by car only since the road was built. The landscape along the way is exceptionally lovely. One arrives at the village square, from which narrow streets wind down to the beach. Jardim do Mar consists of a new and an old district. In the old part (diagonally to the right from the village square), one can still see the traditional one-room stone houses with just one door and usually no windows. This "old town" seems rather desolate, however, since many doors and windows are boarded up and several houses are crumbling and for the most part appear abandoned. Many of Jardim do Mar's residents originally came from Madeira, returned later, and more or less built the new part of Jardim do Mar next to the old. One quickly reaches the sea by following the sign marked *Centro de Saúde.* The focus of social life is a small café with a terrace found on the way there.

Language

Although Madeira's population was formed by a mixture of different nations, Portuguese is the only language spoken; words of other languages and "created" words hardly exist. Foreign language number one is, of course, English, since relations between Madeira and England were once very close *(→History)*. In Funchal and the larger towns, Madeirans who have anything to do with tourists all speak English: waiters, taxi drivers, shop and bank employees, etc. Some Madeirans also speak French, Spanish, or German, languages which the older generation learned during their emigration. In Funchal there are three language schools. Young Madeirans learn at least English and French at school or university, and some also learn German. Menus, information and signs are, as a rule, in English and often also in French and German.

Levadas

The canals lacing the whole island are called *levadas* in Portuguese. The verb *levar* means "lead, carry or bring": the levadas transport water from the rainy north to the dry south *(→Climate)*. The levadas are U-shaped in cross section and may be up to 1 metre (3¼ feet) wide and 30 to 80 cm deep (1 to 2½ feet). They lie open in the ground and are made of stone and limestone. Most levadas originate in the north, where there is an adequate water supply all year, and flow to the south, where there is sometimes no water during the summer. Along their course, there are numerous outlets and sluices that supply the surrounding fields with water. Most levadas are passable and are ideally suited to walking; thus one hardly notices the island's tremendous gradients, since levadas climb (or drop) only about 1 metres per kilometre (½ mile). Levadas are vitally important for Madeira's people: not only do they control irrigation, they also provide Funchal with drinking

The name of this city is Jardim do Mar, which means "garden of the sea," and rightfully so

water. In addition, they serve as footpaths to houses scattered across the slopes, playgrounds for children, and as a place to wash clothes. Thus the importance of leaving levadas undisturbed and clean should be apparent to hikers.

The History of the Levadas

Shortly after the island's discovery, settlers began constructing the first canals. Moorish slaves, having gained experience in canal building in their homelands, took over planning and implementation, while black slaves cut courses through the mountains. It was very hard work which claimed many lives. The slaves often knelt directly above chasms or were even lowered down cliffs in baskets if there was not enough room to kneel. They used simple, even primitive tools to build the canals miles in length: hoes, iron rods, hammers, etc. had to suffice. The use of animals or machines was and is out of the question.

From the beginning, the water was communal property, and landowners were prohibited from obstructing the repair or construction of levadas on their land. Due to increased sugar cane trade, even greater quantities of water were needed for planting and processing. Expansion of the levada system was expedited by investments on the part of landowners and subventions by the government until 1680. Then construction declined with the sugar cane trade. From the early 19th century, the state took over construction of large projects, since private parties lacked sufficient funds. The introduction of the *Codigo Civil,* or civil code, however, changed all that. Water, like land, became private property and could be sold. This led to abuse, wild speculation, and blackmailing of small farmers, who responded with protests and revolts. In the 1940's, large and important levadas were nationalised, and today only smaller ones are still privately owned. Levada workers are state employees.

The Water Distribution System

Spring owners and water lessees, called *Heréus,* have formed societies responsible for the administration and control of levadas. These societies meet regularly, coordinate the "schedule for water distribution," and appoint a *levadeiro,* the waterkeeper. The levadeiro distributes water, checks and cleans canals, and mediates disputes, which frequently arise between lessees. The levadeiro's position is very important and laden with responsibility. Water is channelled off into the lessee's fields through small sluices, which are sometimes no more than little gates across branching ditches. Pollution, clogging, and frequent water theft are the main problems facing the water societies and levadeiros. Water fees are used to repair levadas. The water distribution system is complicated and has developed over the course of centuries.

Levada Statistics

Information on the total length of the levadas varies from several hundred to 5,000 km (3,000 miles), depending on if side canals and branches are included or not. There is a total of 3,300 metres of tunnels (10,791 feet), which are anywhere from 4 to 800 metres long (13 to 2616 feet). Water flow in levadas lies between 12 and

30 litres per second (3 to 8 gallons), depending on size. The only levada not level with the ground level is the *Levada das 25 Fontes* near Rabaçal; it is about waist high to an adult.

Literature

The black-and-white photo book *Impressões da Madeira Antiga* by Luis de Sousa Melo and Susan E. Farrow (about 1500$00) has appeared only in Portuguese, but the historical photographs make it worthwhile in spite of language difficulties. For plant lovers and botanists, a book on the plants and flowers of Madeira by L. O. Franquinho and A. da Costa is recommended reading. This is the most comprehensive key (with photos) to the flora, with systematic and common names in 6 languages. Aside from names, the books by Giudo de Monterey (Madeira, the Flower Island), about 1400$00 and Rui Vieira (Flowers of Madeira), around 1000$00 offer more information, but do not concentrate on species descriptions. All books are in several languages, some of them are available only on Madeira.

Machico

This city, allegedly named after the Englishman Machim *(→History)*, lies on a green bay right next to the Atlantic. It is said that Zarco and Tristão Vaz also landed here when they discovered Madeira. Today, Machico is, after Funchal, the second most important tourist centre and second largest city. The busy centre of town, the plazas with their sidewalk cafés, and people strolling on the beach give it a lively and metropolitan yet laid-back atmosphere found otherwise only in Funchal. Vacationers from the nearby holiday centre *Matur* contribute to the flair. The 14,000 residents make their living from agriculture, fishing, and, of course, tourism. Machico is divided into halves by a river. On one side are located the centre with the main church, courthouse, shops, marketplaces, and triangular fort, and on the other are the fishermen's quarter and residential area.

Machico / **History**

Machico was founded shortly after Madeira's discovery. Tristão Vaz made Machico the main port of his half of the island, granted to him by the Portuguese king. Soon thereafter, a chapel was built on the site where Vaz is said to have found Machim's grave. The *Capela de Cristo* is called *Capela dos Milagres* today and the original form has not been preserved since floods destroyed it several times *(→Machico/Sights)*. The discoverers were not the only ones to find Machico's bay a good place to lay anchor; the pirates used it as well. For this reason, two forts were built here to protect the populace. Also during the Portuguese civil war *(→History)*, these forts were the scene of bloody battles.

Machico was an important region for the production of sugar cane. At the beginning of the century, there were several sugar cane processing plants, which are closed today. A fish cannery also closed down due to lacking profitability. Today, fish are auctioned at the *Lota,* or market hall right on the shore.

Machico / **Sights**

The changing history of Machico is made most clear by the church, chapel, and two forts, which characterise the town.

The original *Capela de São Roque* from 1489 no longer exists; it was destroyed and rebuilt several times. In its current form, it stands at the edge of town toward Santa Cruz. The azulejos of the 18th century are especially worth seeing. The church of *Nossa Senhora da Conceição* was built in the 15th century, but thereafter, it was repeatedly destroyed and rebuilt. Of note are the double ogive gate with marble columns from the 15th century, the organ — a gift from King D. Manuel I — and the side chapels. There is a monument to the discoverer of Madeira and founder of Machico, Tristão Vaz Teixeira, on the church square which was dedicated in 1972.

The triangular *Forte de Nossa Senhora do Amparo,* built to protect the city from pirates who found it a simple matter to come ashore here from the bay, was built in 1706. Today, it houses the *Guarda Fiscal,* the border and customs police; in the future, the fort is to be made into a museum. The *Forte de São João Baptista* lies across the river and was built in 1708. On this side of the river, one also finds the 15th century *Capela do Milagres.* This chapel was given the name "Chapel of Miracles" because a portrait of Christ was swept out to sea by a storm tide in 1803, where it was miraculously found by an American ship and brought back to the island.

Machico / **Practical Information**

Accommodation: The Residencial with its restaurant "O Facho" is located directly next to the sports field near the beach, 13 rooms, double occupancy 4500$00, Tel: 96 27 86, 96 45 36. The Residencial "Machico" is just across from it, 6 rooms, double occupancy 4500$00. Reservations are recommended in both cases. On the road to Caniçal, one will find the residencial "O Econdidinho," Tel: 96 24 42. Its 10 rooms are somewhat less expensive than the centrally located residencials (double occupancy 3000$00). The four-star hotel "D. Pedro Baía" is more luxurious and impossible to overlook at the edge of town (toward Funchal), Tel: 96 23 21, Fax: 96 38 89, double occupancy from about 14,000$00, single occupancy from about 11,000$00. Further accommodations are of course available at *Matur* on Água de Pena, Tel: 96 23 21.

Banks: The three banks are located around the main church and church square.

Car Rental: In Machico itself, there are no car rental agencies. About 3 km (1½ miles) away at the holiday centre *Matur,* two companies are represented in the Centro Comercial Matur: Bravacar, Tel: 96 33 58; Interrent Rent-a-Car, Tel: 96 23 83.

Cinema: A cinema is located on R. do Ribeirinho, Tel: 96 26 59.

Festivals: From the night of October 8th to the 9th, Machico celebrates *O Senhor dos Milagres* with a procession. It commemorates the rescue of a crucifix which was swept out to sea in 1803 from the Christ Chapel, as it was then called, and later recovered by a ship.

Medical Care: The hospital *Policlínica,* Rua do Ribeirinho, Tel: 96 20 06; pharmacy *Farmácia Zarco,* Rua da Ávore 13, Tel: 96 21 97.

Restaurants: There is no lack of restaurants in Machico. Local cuisine at reasonable prices is served at "O General" at Rua General A. Teixeira de Aguiar 91, Tel: 96 39 36, around 300 metres (980 feet) behind the main church (when looking from the shore). Seafood and other local cuisine at somewhat higher prices is served outdoors in a lively atmosphere at "Mercado Verlho," Rua General A. T. de Aguiar, near the fort, Tel: 96 23 70. On the road to Caniçal is the restaurant "O Escondidinho," Tel: 96 24 42, also serving local dishes at normal prices. Its unusual feature is a mossy, plant-covered wall with water continually running over it. Somewhat outside of town is "S. Cristovão," a restaurant with good, reasonably priced food and a unique view (at least during clear weather) of the Desertas and Machico from the roofed terrace. One follows ER 101 towards Portela until a sign appears to the right, pointing the way to "S. Cristovão" (near the church in Caramanchão), Tel: 96 24 44.

Shopping: The little shopping centre *Centro Comercial Avenida* on Rua da Amargura has clothing, shoes, and sporting goods. There is a supermarket directly adjacent. Fresh foods are best purchased at the marketplace, which is right on the beach. Wine, beer, and other alcoholic beverages are available at decent prices at *Cervejaria Estrela Azul* at Rua General A. Teixeira de Aguiar 12. Souvenirs and handicrafts are sold at a small shop in the *Residencial O Escondidinho* on the road to Caniçal.

Sports and Recreation: One can play tennis and swim at the holiday centre *Matur* and at Hotel "D. Pedro."

Swimming: Machico has a black-sand beach. Other possibilities are the Hotel D. Pedro and *Matur* swimming pools.

Tourist Information: Machico is the only town besides Funchal that has its own tourist information office. It is located on Rua do Ribeirinho and is open from Monday to Friday from 9:30 am to 12:30 pm and 2 to 5:30 pm; on Saturday from 9:30 to noon, Tel: 96 27 12. The booklet "Machico" by Zita Cardoso, also containing walking and hiking routes, is available here.

Transportation: Bus numbers 23, 53 and 113 are in operation to Funchal. They also stop at the airport.

Important Addresses: Police: Rua da Banda D'Alem (in the residential portion of the city), Tel: 96 25 74.

Madalena do Mar

The good coastal road ER 213 ends at Madalena do Mar, which is about 4 km (2½ miles) from Ponta do Sol.

The village, remote and thus especially tranquil even today, extends along the rocky shoreline. One cannot miss the small village centre if one follows the sign to *Centro de Saúde.* At the centre, one finds the chapel *Santa Maria Madalena,* after which the settlement was named, a bar, and a telephone booth. Following this street, one soon sees a sign "Restaurante," indicating the seafood restaurant "Arpoeta" 300 metres (980 feet) farther along.

An interesting history surrounds this modest little village:

The first settler is said to have been a man of uncertain origins, who was called "Henrique o Alemão" — Henry the German — by Madeirans of his day. Zarco received a royal order to grant him land that he could make arable. Neither D. Henrique nor King D. Afonso V mentioned the name of the grantee in their grant deed of 1457, in which they confirmed his possession of the land. This man was allegedly Ladislaus III, King of Poland and Hungary. Ladislaus III disappeared after losing the battle of Varna in 1444, a campaign he led against the Turkish sultan, although a legal peace treaty already existed. According to the legend, Ladislaus

The market in Funchal: exotic fish can be purchased during the early morning hours

was tormented by a guilty conscience after his treason, and he undertook a pilgrimage to the Holy Land. A few years later, he surfaced in Portugal and offered the Portuguese King his services as pioneer to settle newly discovered territory. He married a Portuguese woman, founded Madalena do Mar and built the chapel of *Santa Maria Madalena*. He died while returning to Madalena (which at that time was accessible only by ship) when his boat was caught in a landslide below Cabo Girão. It is historically not 100 percent certain that Henrique o Alemão and Ladislaus III, King of Poland and Hungary, were one and the same person. A painting from the church at Madalena, exhibited today in the museum *Arte Sacra* (→*Funchal*), depicts not only the meeting of Saint Anna and Saint Joachim, but is also supposedly a portrait of Ladislaus and his wife Senhorinha Anes.

Maps

A map of Madeira (with city map of Funchal) and Porto Santo can be obtained free of charge at tourist information offices on the islands (→*Tourist Information*). A map of Madeira (with Porto Santo and city map of Funchal) with a scale of 1:75,000 has been published by Kümmerly and Frey Publishers, which is a better map for driving than the one given out by tourist information offices; roads are colour coded according to size/quality. This map appeared in cooperation with the firm "Districultural, Sacavém, Portugal," and is available only on Madeira (about 800$00; it's worth comparing prices).

Markets

Markets are located in halls made for that purpose, with permanent stands. Fruit, vegetables, meat, fish, and flowers can be bought fresh and are usually less expensive at the markets than in supermarkets. In the larger towns such as Funchal, Machico, Ribeira Brava, Câmara de Lobos and Santa Cruz, markets take place daily, although the selection is larger and more diverse during weekends. Prices are fixed and given per kilogram (2.2 lbs.). Therefore, bargaining is thus usually futile. The biggest market is, of course, in Funchal, and is called the *Mercado dos Lavradores* (farmer's market). It is located on Rua Latino Coelho in the old town and is a large, two-story structure with an open inner courtyard. During the week, only the permanent stands are open, while on Fridays and Saturdays the aisles and inner courtyard are also used for selling. The fish market is right next to the fruit and vegetable sections.

A visit to the *Mercado dos Lavradores* is an unforgettable experience for anyone visiting Madeira: a very special atmosphere is created by the variety and quantity of fruit and flowers, freshly caught tuna and espadas, the hectic bustle of business, and the wide array of smells and souvenirs, for instance wickerwork. Don't miss it! Late on Thursday or Friday evenings, one should stroll around the *Mercado* grounds; farmers are already unloading their goods in preparation for the next market day. Early in the morning, the selection of fish is the largest, and the sight of so many colourful, freshly-caught fish surely makes up for having to get up so early.

Hours: Monday to Thursday and Saturday, 7 am to 4 pm (fish from 7 am to 2 pm); Friday from 7 am to 8 pm (fish until 2 pm).

Medical Care

Medical care on Madeira is good, and the technical equipment in hospitals corresponds to the central European standards. Most doctors speak English.

Ambulance service is available by contacting the Red Cross (Tel: 20 000) or dialling the emergency number 115.

There is a state hospital in Funchal near the Carlton Hotel on Avenida Luis de Camões, Tel: 4 21 11. In addition, there are private clinics: Clínica Sta. Catarina, Rua 5 de Outubro, Tel: 2 01 27, and Centro Médico da Sé, Rua das Murcas 42, Tel: 3 01 27.

To receive treatment at a state hospital, one needs a medical insurance form for travel abroad, which one can take to the regional health administration and receive a Portuguese insurance coupon booklet for medical treatment. The booklet is available at the Direcção Regional de Saúde Pública, Rua das Pretas 1 in Funchal. Of course in emergencies, one will receive treatment immediately. At private hospitals, one must pay oneself. Prices are comparable to those in central Europe, so it is a good idea to inquire about cost in advance.

Minor injuries are treated free of charge at a *Centro de Saúde*. These "health centres" can be found in every village; there are signs indicating the way there. They are usually open from 8 am to 8 pm.

Medication

Any special prescriptions or medications should, of course, be brought along, otherwise one can find the usual over-the-counter medications at most pharmacies. It is advisable to take along bandages, iodine, medications for seasickness and diarrhoea, insect sting ointment, and disinfectant.

→*Pharmacies, Medical Care*

Monte

Monte lies slightly over 6 km (3½ miles) north of and 550 metres (1,800 feet) higher than Funchal. The community has been independent since May 14, 1568. In the last century as well, Monte was a favourite tourist destination and the location of some of the most beautiful hotels and villas. The proximity to Funchal, the wonderful mountain location (after all, Monte means "mountain"), the tranquillity and picturesque view of Funchal and the sea make it a very attractive place.

Monte / **Sights**

The church *Nossa Senhora do Monte* is often visited by pilgrims and the faithful; the image of the Holy Virgin on the church's high altar is revered and worshipped. Once, it is told, the Holy Virgin appeared as a shepherd to a girl. One of the island's first chapels stood on this site from 1470 to 1741, when the construction of the church was begun. This was, however, destroyed in an earthquake and had to be rebuilt; it was christened in its present form in 1818.

Monte's centre is the plaza Largo da Fonte, shaded by old plane trees, where a fountain chapel and several bars, restaurants, and souvenir shops are also located. From here, one can explore the lovely city park, opened in 1899, which begins under the bridge and stretches almost without interruption up to the church. Up until 50 years ago, a cog railway crossed this bridge and connected Monte with Funchal; there were no tourist buses at that time. One can only imagine how difficult the planning and construction of this railway must have been. Unfortunately, operating the cog railway was not without accidents; thus, it was dismantled in 1943 and the materials were sold after 50 years of service.

The famed basket-sleds or *Carro de Cesto* are still in operation, so far with no accidents! The basket-sled drivers wait below the church's outer stairs, always dressed in white and wearing straw hats. The trip starts here, and the Carreiros steer, push, and brake on the steep, bumpy way down the valley to Funchal. One trip to Livramento costs 1250$00, and all the way to Funchal is 1800$00 per person.

Sadly, the *Grand Hotel Belmonte* is no longer in business; it has the best location in town. There is also a school on its grounds. The grounds constitute a big, beautiful park, which may open soon to tourists.

The Quinta do Monte park or *Quinta de Nossa Senhora de Conceição* on the way from Monte to Barbosas is especially worth seeing. In front of the quinta, one can buy an admission ticket (200$00) at the *Old Monte Taverne,* which is fashioned to look like an old pirate tavern. Winston Churchill was often a guest at the 200-year-old quinta, whose garden is a gem of the art of landscaping. Open Tuesday to Friday from 10 am to 6 pm.

Monte / **Surroundings**

To the right behind Monte's church, there is a paved road leading up to *Terreiro da Luta.* It is steep, so this walk takes about 30 minutes. Of course, one can also go by bus or taxi. It is worthwhile to enjoy the view from the quinta's "Esplanada" Garden with its bronze Zarco monument as early in the day as possible. The no longer existent cog railway came up here as well.

A bit farther along, one finds the 5.5-metre tall (18 foot) marble monument to *Nossa Senhora da Paz* and the chapel. This monument commemorates the end of World War I and was dedicated in 1927. The rosary around the monument is made of large stones, dragged to Terreiro da Luta from the beach in a prayer procession.

Later, as a symbol of peace, the stones were joined with a chain from a warship sunk during the First World War. On October 15th, a procession and folk festival with fireworks takes place in honour of the Holy Virgin.

Excursions to Monte including a sled ride can be booked at travel agencies. It is a simple matter, though, to take the bus (no. 22) from Funchal. One can return either by bus or basket-sled. By car, take E 103 from Funchal to Monte.

Nudism

Swimming nude is officially prohibited in Portugal, and due to the lack of beaches on Madeira, there is hardly the opportunity to do so anyway. Obviously, swimwear is mandatory at hotels and public pools.

On Porto Santo, nude bathing and sunbathing is simply not practised. One should be aware that one is a guest and should respect local customs and values.

Paúl da Serra

The high plain of Madeira is not only the largest area of flat ground on the island, it is also the least populated. Although the dimensions are by no means overwhelming (6 km/3½ miles long and 4 km/2½ miles wide at 1,500 metres/4,900 feet elevation), this landscape does have something "endless" about it. The low, sparse vegetation and numerous boulders on the high plain where sheep and goats are the only inhabitants create the impression of desolate steppes. In the 1960's, Paúl da Serra was supposed to become the site of Madeira's airport, but the ever-present fog, rough winds, and high elevation put an end to these plans. It is used only as pasture for sheep, goats, and sometimes horses. The harsh climate and shortage of water prohibit any other agricultural use. The plain was formed by a volcanic eruption after the birth of the island itself. The seclusion of Paúl da Serra is interrupted twice a year: once for sheep shearing and once for the Rallye Vinho da Madeira.

Paúl do Mar

The most interesting thing about Paúl do Mar is getting there: a serpentine road winding down and through a mountain, opening onto a view of a verdant bay that is expansive by Madeiran standards. Like Jardim do Mar, Paúl do Mar has only been accessible by land since the road was built. Due to centuries of isolation, a special atmosphere evolved in Paúl do Mar, which can even be perceived today. The people are reserved, and tourists are cause for confused glances and whispering. The apparel of Paúl residents is distinct from that of other Madeirans. Even today, the old women wear lace-trimmed head scarves called *mantilha*. In this village, the emigration rate is very high.

The People of Madeira

The origin of Madeira's population can be traced back to different peoples. The archipelago was unpopulated when Zarco and Vaz Teixeira discovered it. Soon thereafter, the island was settled by the Portuguese (→*History*). For the purpose of building the →*levadas* and cultivating sugar cane, slaves from Africa, South America, and the Canary Islands were imported. Close political and economic relations with England brought many English settlers to the island. The ethnic profile of Madeira is created by the descendants of all of these nations. There are fair-skinned blondes as well as black and dark-skinned Madeirans, and of course many who are rather melodramatically called "Zarco's Heirs." Although each group, naturally, has left its mark on the culture, it is decidedly Portuguese.

Madeira is a densely populated island, with a total population of around 270,000. Overpopulation, countless economic crises, and the subdivision of land due to inheritance laws forced thousands to emigrate to South America, the United States, or the Portuguese colonies. Especially during the crisis-ridden 19th century, emigration took on such massive proportions that the authorities forbade it. Many Madeirans then fled their "flower island" by rowing out to sea in fishing boats, there to wait for rescue by passing ocean liners. Between 1835 and 1855 some 40,000 Madeirans are said to have emigrated, with another 39,000 leaving between 1890 and 1910. Many residents still emigrate today in order to escape unemployment and poverty. In some of the more remote villages, one notices the appearance of abandonment and a populace composed predominantly of the elderly. Young Madeirans are drawn to Funchal, where they work in hotels and restaurants instead of cultivating the labour-intensive terraced fields at home as their parents did. Opportunities for study are also limited on the archipelago. There is a university in Funchal, but not all subjects are offered, and lecturers must often be flown in from the mainland. For this reason alone, many young Madeirans prefer to live on the Continent.

Pharmacies

These are called *farmácia* in Portuguese. There are many of them in Funchal, and in every mid-sized town, there is at least one at the centre. Lists of pharmacies offering 24-hour service are posted in the pharmacies; this information can also be obtained by calling 166 or asking at the hotel reception. English is usually understood at the pharmacies. Prescription medications must be paid for at once, but one should save the receipt so that these expenses can be reimbursed by one's health insurance at home.

Business Hours: Monday to Friday from 9 am to 1 pm and 3 to 7 pm.
→*Medical Care*

Photography

Madeira provides amateur and professional photographers alike with countless photographic motifs. One should take plenty of film along. Film and accessories are available on Madeira, but are considerably more expensive. Film is less expensive at camera shops than at souvenir shops or kiosks.

Pico do Arieiro

At 1,818 metres (5,944 feet) in elevation, this is the second highest mountain on Madeira. Road ER 202 leads directly to the restaurant and the state-owned luxury hotel "Pousada do Pico do Arieiro."

On foot, one can best discover Madeira's mountain world on the path from Arieiro to Pico Ruivo (→*Hiking, Excursions, Pico Ruivo*). The weather at these altitudes is often strikingly different than at lower elevations. The valleys may be fogged-in and gloomy while the peaks lie above the clouds and one is surrounded by clear blue skies. However, one should avoid setting out in foggy or rainy weather. Sunsets from the top of Pico do Arieiro are spectacular. The play of light and colour on the evening clouds will make for a unique memory of Madeira (especially in autumn).

Accommodation/Restaurant: "Pousada do Pico do Arieiro," Tel: 4 81 88, 41 81 98, reservations required.

Transportation: Bus no. 103 (toward Boaventura) to Poiso, then by taxi.

Pico Ruivo

Madeira's highest peak at 1,861 metres (6,085 feet) can only be reached on foot. A forest hut just under the summit offers a simple accommodation with no luxuries. Food is not provided; the employees just supply bedding. Reservations are mandatory at "Quinta Vigia" (→*Quintas and Parks*), since the government employees do not allow visitors without a reservation card to stay the night, even if there are vacancies. Hikers can reach Pico Ruivo ("Red Peak") from Madeira's second highest mountain, Pico do Arieiro, along a good trail (→*Hiking*). Suppliers bringing beverages to the guest facilities at Pico Ruivo use the easier route from Achada do Teixeira. It takes a little over an hour to reach the peak along this paved pathway. Visitors to Madeira should allow plenty of time for the walk to Pico Ruivo, since it offers unexpected and ever-surprising views of Madeira's truly overwhelming mountain world. The entire island can be seen from the summit. To the west, one sees the long, flat ridge of Paúl da Serra; fog often wells up mysteriously from the valleys in between — a simply unforgettable experience.

Police

In case of theft, traffic accidents, etc. the *Polícia de Segurança Pública* can be reached by calling the emergency number 115 (→*Emergencies*). The foreign language abilities of the police are rather limited, however. Therefore, one should ask at the hotel or consulate for help when speaking to the police.

Politics

Portugal has been a parliamentary, democratic republic consisting of 22 districts since the revolution of April 25, 1974 that dissolved the authoritarian Salazar state (→History). Madeira, Porto Santo, the Desertas and the Selvagens make up the district of Funchal. Madeira and the Azores are autonomous provinces. The regional government of the autonomous province is answerable to the Regional Assembly. The head of the regional government is appointed by the Minister of the Republic. The autonomous regions send representatives to the Lisbon parliament. The current Portuguese government is dominated by the conservative Social Democratic People's Party (PSD), whose incumbent prime minister is Anibal Cavaco Silva; the state president is Mario Soares, a socialist. Madeira's incumbent president is Alberto João Jardim.

When Portugal joined the EC in 1986, it had grave consequences for the Madeiran economy as well (→Economy).

An unforgettable experience: the sunset as seen from the summit of Pico do Arieiro

Ponta de São Lourenço

The extreme eastern point of Madeira is a desolate piece of land whose sparse vegetation and shimmering yellow-red cliffs plunging straight down to the sea have an attraction all their own. This uninhabited area is used by Madeirans as hunting grounds, since innumerable rabbits live here. The small peninsula was named by Zarco after his ship, the "São Lourenço," with which he circumnavigated the island. At the end of ER 101-3 there is a good spot for picnicking and starting point for walks. One can walk out to the end of the east point from here *(→ Hiking)*. The outlying island *Ilhéu de Agostinho* is uninhabited, and there is a lighthouse on *Ilhéu da Fora.*

Ponta Delgada

This region, characterised in the past by vineyards and sugar cane, attracted many prosperous families, who built stately villas which now attest to former wealth of this region. Since the middle of the 16th century, the *Arraial do Senhor Jesus,* beloved all over the island, has been celebrated here on the first Sunday in September.

Ponta do Pargo

The land surrounding *Ponta do Pargo* is flatter than most other places on the island. From the lighthouse, one has a superb view of cliffs and the ocean, which even the grazing cattle seem to enjoy. The lighthouse is reached by following signs marked *Farol* from the centre of the village. Next to the church, the 15th-century *Capela de São Pedro,* there is a new, reasonably priced restaurant and café.

Ponta do Sol

Coming from Ribeira Brava, the road to Ponta do Sol leads through several tunnels directly along the coast. The coastline here is very rugged and mountainous. The little village is spread out up the mountain and has a centre of narrow, crooked streets. At the entrance to town is the police station, located above the tunnel. Turning right before the tunnel and following the *Centro de Saúde* signs, one immediately reaches the village's main street. Located here are the *pharmacy,* a *minimercado,* the only *restaurant and cafe,* and *the village church, Nossa Senhora da Luz* (Our Lady of Light). Very simple accommodation without breakfast but with bathrooms are available at the guest house "Senhor Manuel da Praça," Rua Agosto Teixeira 43, Tel: 97 25 39, costing 1500$00 to 2000$00 per night. The house is right across from the church.

The church roof is of Spanish-Moorish origin, and the wooden ceiling is painted with events from the life of Christ. The baptismal font with its green ceramic tiles is especially remarkable. Construction on the church began in the 15th century; Ponta do Sol was founded in 1440. Going uphill, the street soon becomes cobbled and impassable for cars. On the left is the house of American writer *John dos Passos'* ancestors. His grandfather, Manuel Joaquim dos Passos, left Ponta do Sol at the age of 18 to emigrate to the United States. John dos Passos was born in Chicago in 1896. His anti-war novel "Three Soldiers" made him famous, and his novel "Manhattan Transfer," a socially critical book set in New York, impressed other writers, such as Döblin and Sartre, with its differential narrative techniques. Further, he wrote a trilogy of novels on North American society ("The 42nd Parallel," "1919" and "High Finance"). John dos Passos visited Ponta do Sol for the last time on July 20, 1960, as noted on a commemorative plaque on what is now the local administrative office. He died on September 28, 1970 in Baltimore.

The paved street uphill to the right from the dos Passos house leads to the post office, which is open Monday to Friday from 9 am to 12:30 pm and 2:30 to 5:30 pm.

Portela

For the traveller, Portela is actually only interesting as a viewpoint and rest stop. The overwhelming, panorama view from 670 metres (2,191 feet) above Machico, the cliffs of Penha de Aguia (590 metres/1,929 feet), Porto da Cruz and Santo da Serra are worth a short stop. Two restaurants, the "Casa da Portela" and "Portela a vista," offer refreshing breaks.

Porto da Cruz

At the foot of the eagle cliffs, *Penha de Aguia* (590 metres/1,929 feet), lies Porto da Cruz with direct access to the ocean. The area surrounding it is characterised by sugar cane and vineyards. The last sugar cane mill in operation is located here, and with some luck, one can observe it at work during March and April. On the way to the rocky beach, one passes the small centre of town with its church, a minimercado, and taxi stand. Bygone glory from the sugar cane era clings to Porto da Cruz: old villas, once magnificent, now stand in disrepair. Going along the beach road in town, one encounters the only restaurant, the "Penha de Ave." Straight ahead a bit farther, behind the soccer field, is the old *sugar cane factory,* whose steam machines are from the last century. The cane is used to make a kind of schnapps, *aguardente.* The factory is in operation only 20 days a year at sugar cane harvest time in March and April. Aguardente is manufactured for consumption only on Madeira, though small quantities are still exported to the Canary Islands. Daily production is around 3,000 litres (780 gallons). The sugar-rich stems are repeatedly pressed then finally used to stoke the fires under the steam kettles. The juice is purified and boiled. After crystalisation, brown sugar is left over and the remaining liquid is fermented.

Porto Moniz

The road leading from Paúl da Serra or from the direction of Santa to Porto Moniz winds in serpentines down the coast and offers a fantastic view of the town from above. On the slopes and in town there are many terraced fields bordered by *urze*, a dry heather hedge intended to protect them from the strong north wind. All year long, Porto Moniz is a quiet place not heavily frequented by holiday travellers, due to its location on the northern coast and the resulting cold, wet weather (except in summer). During the summer months, Porto Moniz awakens from its enchanted slumber; the weather is stable and good and the natural swimming pool fills with visitors. Natural cliff formations on the coast create small pools (which are in part concrete reinforced) of various shapes and sizes, from which one may also swim out into the ocean. This summer attraction is the reason for the relatively large number of accomodations and Madeira's only campground. In the near future, another hotel and a restaurant will be built.

The considerable number of modern villas and houses were built by emigrants from Porto Moniz who here invest money earned abroad and may only return home for holidays. The quite small population of 500 is not surprising, because even today Porto Moniz has a high rate of emigration. Residents make their living chiefly in agriculture, mainly wine grapes and potatoes (tropical plants like bananas do not do well here).

Porto Moniz was founded by Francisco Moniz, the husband of one of Zarco's grand-daughters.

Porto Moniz / **Practical Information**

Accommodation: Madeira's only campground lies directly on the coast. It is clean, inexpensive, rather new, and has well-maintained sanitary facilities. Unfortunately, there is no protection from the cutting wind that often arises on this coast. At the "Cachalote" restaurant's swimming pool, one can rent a room, "Alojamento Rodriguez," Tel: 85 22 33, double occupancy 3500$00.

At the other end of the beach are two residencials: Residencial "Orca," Tel: 85 23 59, double occupancy from 4950$00 to 5500$00, single between 3850$00 and 4400$00; Residencial "Calhau," Tel: 85 21 04, double occupancy 4000$00, single 3000$00. In summer, reservations are absolutely necessary!

Private, newly renovated rooms with their own bathrooms are available near the church: "Jomar-Alojamento," Sítio da Igreja, Tel: 85 22 78, double occupancy from 2000$00. Bargaining is possible, the rule of thumb is "the longer the stay, the cheaper the rates." (Directions: take the small street between the bank and the church up to the right, then the first small, cobblestone street to the left, and ring the bell at the first door on the left.) Two other places offering accommodation are located in the village of Santa, about 4 km (2½ miles) from Porto Moniz: "Residencial do Norte," Sítio do Cabo-Salão, Tel: 85 22 54, 8 apartments with kitchen, bath, living room and bedroom for 4000$00, down from them are a restaurant/café and minimercado (the way is marked when coming from Porto Moniz); "Pensão Residencial Fernandes" is in Santa right across from the church, Tel: 85 21 36, double occupancy with breakfast 3000$00, double occupancy with kitchenette 4000$00, single room 1500$00.

Banks: Two banks are located near the church at the entrance to town.

Festivals: Santa Maria Madalena is celebrated on July 22.

Restaurants: Restaurant "Cachalote" with a view of the ocean (built on a cliff), turn right along the coast (coming from the church), just next to one of the natural swimming pools. The restaurant and café "Fernandes" lies directly to the right of this, large, pleasant interior, typical Madeiran food, relatively high in price. To the left seen from the entrance to town is a modern, somewhat more expensive restaurant, "Polo Norte," on the coast. There are two other restaurants at the hotels "Calahau" and "Orca" (→Accommodation).

Shopping: There is a minimercado near the church on the street leading to the beach.

Swimming: Two natural swimming pools are located in front of the hotel/restaurants "Calhau" and "Cachalote," admission is around 55$00.

Porto Santo

The small, neighbouring island of Porto Santo is Madeira's natural counterpart. Porto Santo is 20 minutes by plane or 1½ hours by ferry, the "Pátria." Rough seas may, however, spoil the fun of a boat ride for some people.

Porto Santo is about 40 km (24 miles) northeast of Madeira and is only 42 square kilometres (16 square miles) in area, 14 km (8½ miles) long and 6 km (3½ miles) wide. The island is flatter and less densely vegetated and populated than the big island. About 5,000 people live here, 2,000 of them in Vila Baleira.

The main attraction is certainly the 7-kilometre long (4 mile) beach of fine, yellow-gold sand, which they say even has healing properties.

Water temperature varies with season (as does air temperature) between 16 and 22 °C (61 and 72 °F).

In general, the climate is drier than on Madeira, with rainfall chiefly confined to the winter months (→Climate). Thus, the vegetation looks quite desolate in summer. There are thick pine and cedar woods only on *Pico do Castello*. This is the centrally located, conical, watershed mountain where in past centuries, inhabitants sought refuge from pirates. The mountain was reforested a few years ago.

The many outlying islands and cliffs each have names and interesting characteristics. *Ilhéu de Cima* and *Ilhéu de Ferro,* for instance, have grottoes with stalactites and stalagmites.

The island suffers from lack of water, but possesses several excellent mineral water springs. There is a bottling facility in Vila Baleira on the main road across from

PORTO SANTO

ILHÉU DE FERRO

Camacha

Fonte da Areia *

Pico do Castelo

Pico do Facho

Serra de Dentro

Lapeiras

Campo de Cima

Tanque

Serra de Fora

Pedras Pretas

Capela de Graça

Campo de Baixo

PORTO SANTO
Vila Baleira

to Funchal

Ponta

Ponta da Calheta *

ILHÉU DE BAIXO

Ferry

ILHÉU DAS CENOURAS

ILHÉU DE CIMA

N

0   3 km

the campground. The clinking of bottles can be heard at some distance, if the 50-year-old machines aren't taking a break. An excursion to *Fonte da Areia,* the sand spring, is worthwhile not only to try to water, but also to get an impression of the heavily dissected northern coast.

Porto Santo is a popular excursion and holiday destination for Madeirans, and is becoming increasingly popular among European tourists in conjunction with a holiday on Madeira. The number of accommodation will soon be increased in order to fully capitalise on tourism. The whole range of accommodation options is available.

The technological progress of the 20th century has also made its mark on this small island. The airport opened in 1960, whose long runway also served as Madeira's airport for 4 years before the big island, with great effort, built its own. Today, Porto Santo's airport is used by NATO and for daily traffic between islands. Earlier, wind energy was used to grind grain; today, wind generators produce electricity to do this and other jobs. This rather new project is exemplary of "clean" energy production. The oil spill in 1990 was somewhat less clean. The cliffs and rocks on the eastern coast are still smeared with black oil. A large-scale clean-up was undertaken to remove as much oil from the beach as possible.

The sand beach was, fortunately, spared and remained untouched by the oil catastrophe.

Porto Santo / **Agriculture and Vegetation**

Windmills are characteristic of the island; grain is ground there. The area surrounding *Campo de Cima* and *Campo de Baixo* is flat enough for extensive fields. Farmers have always had to battle with drought and soil erosion; stone walls are intended to hinder the latter. An irrigation system does not exist because water supplies from wells or cisterns are inadequate.

Grapes are cultivated flat on the ground and, due to the abundant sunshine, the vines produce sweet, strong-tasting table grapes and a special Porto Santo wine. Figs require a lot of sun as well and these plants thrive on Porto Santo.

Otherwise, farmers keep cows and sheep and grow vegetables for their own consumption. As a result, the market does not have as great a selection as in Funchal. It is said that originally, the island was forested with tropical hardwood trees, which, like juniper and heather for example, can no longer be found here. Only Pico do Castello is thickly forested. The island's sparse vegetation is dominated by herbs and shrubs.

Porto Santo / **Sights**

Columbus Museum: It seems certain that Columbus was born sometime between August 25 and October 31, 1451 as Cristofero Colombo, son of a master weaver in Genoa. At the early age of 14, he set out to sea as a ship's boy. He worked for several years as a sailor, and went to Lisbon for the first time in 1476. There, in 1479 he married the daughter of Bartolomeu Perestrello, Capitão of Porto Santo Island, and moved with her to the island, where he studied old sailing maps and collected and evaluated the tales and reports of seafarers. At that time, it first occurred to him to try reaching India via the western sea route. His son, Diego, was born in 1480; his wife died sometime between 1482 and 1485.

In 1482, he asked the Portuguese king to support his discovery plans; this, in vain. He turned to the Spanish, French, and English courts for help, but only 10 years later (1492) did he receive financing from Spain's king and queen for his first voyage. With three ships, the Pinta, Niña, and Santa María, Cristobál Colón set out on August 3, 1492. He was knighted, made admiral, and named viceroy of the new lands. On October 12, 1492, after a long journey overshadowed by doubts and a near-mutiny of the superstitious crew, he landed on an island which he named San Salvador. He reached Cuba on October 28, and to his disappointment, found no gold. To prove his success and confirm his discovery of what he believed was India, he enslaved the trusting natives ("brown gold").

Because the "Santa Maria" had sunk, Columbus established the first settlement on Haiti (Hispaniola). In April of the following year, he returned in triumph to Barcelona. Not only did he bring Indio slaves, sweet potatoes, and hammocks, his crew introduced syphilis to Europe, where, thanks to numerous wars and feuds, it rapidly spread over the whole continent. After Pope Alexander VI divided the world into a Portuguese half and a Spanish half, and in spite of the Spanish kings' constant shortage of funds and his own declining reputation, Columbus sailed three more times to the Caribbean (1493, 1498 and 1505), getting as far a Venezuela. On his fourth journey, he finally discovered the gold which he had so desperately sought. The ruthless behaviour of the Spanish conquerors increasingly caused the Indios to resist the "White Gods," and it came to battles. In the first four years after "discovery," over 100,000 Indios died in slavery, of hunger and disease, and in armed conflicts. At the Spanish court, Columbus was held in ill-repute, and he was stripped of his title of viceroy. Amerigo Vespucci called Columbus' discoveries the "New World." His first name gave the recently discovered continent its present name. Until his death, Columbus believed he had reached India. He died after an illness on May 21, 1506 in Valladolid.

At his presumed residence on Porto Santo, his voyages are shown on maps and models of his ships are on display. Various papers document his life. Upon request, tours in English or French are given free of charge. For the 500th anniversary of his discovery of America, there is an abundance of books. The house is open Monday and Wednesday to Saturday, from 10 am to noon and 2 to 5:30 pm; admission is free of charge.

A kind of amphitheatre is being built behind the Columbus house, where folklore performances and festivals can take place.

The modest church *Nossa Senhora de Piedade* at the centre of Vila Baleira dominates the village square. The oldest section of the church, from the 16th century, is the side chapel to the south, which exhibits Gothic features. The even older sections from 1450 and earlier were destroyed by pirates; the current church was rebuilt in the 17th century. Tourists may visit the church only on weekends, before or after church services; otherwise, it is closed.

The chapel *Nossa Senhora da Graça* is seldom open. It is likewise quite plain, and has a lofty position to the east above Vila Baleira.

Porto Santo / **Vila Baleira**

Vila Baleira is the central town and "centre" of the island. Earlier, ferries arrived here, and before the long dock was built, guests were brought by boat from the ferry to shore. In contrast, today one arrives rather unromantically at the large harbour at the east tip of Porto Santo.

One can familiarise oneself with Vila Baleira on a short way. From the pier, go straight ahead to Largo do Pelourinho, past the entrance to *Turismo*. The plaza in front of the courthouse and church is the focal point and place to meet any time of day. One can gain an overview of it from the terrace at the café and restaurant "Baiana."

There are three or four main streets where shops, banks, travel agencies and other important businesses and offices are located. For instance, at the lower end of Rua João Gonçalves Zarco, which runs parallel to the shore, one will find the market; farther up are little shops for all needs, two supermarkets, and the bakery at the corner which is — no exaggeration — the best on the archipelago. Bread, cakes, and coffee in every conceivable form are so delicious and inexpensive that one hardly knows what to try first.

Porto Santo / **Practical Information**

Accommodation: The four-star hotel "Porto Santo" lies somewhat outside town directly on the beach, Tel: 98 23 81/2; double occupancy, with breakfast 13,100$00. Three-star hotel: "Hotel Praia Dourada," Rua Dr. Pedro Lomelino, Vila Baleira, Tel: 98 23 15; double occupancy with breakfast 10,800$00. "Pensão Palmeiras," Avenida Vieira de Castro, Tel: 98 21 12; double occupancy with breakfast 8200$00. "Pensão Zarco," Rua João Gonçalves Zarco, Tel: 98 22 73; double occupancy with kitchen 4800$00. Private apartments can also be rented through Turismo; these are mostly double rooms with kitchen and bath for around 3500$00 in winter and around 4500$00 in summer. One can also inquire directly at "Canção do Mar," Tel: 98 26 03 or 98 23 61 and at "Garten," Tel: 2 14 34 and "Mar Azul," Tel: 2 85 63, both in Funchal.

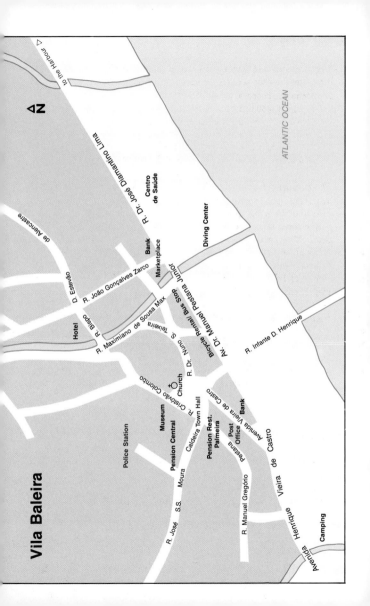

Banks: Two banks are on Avenida Vieira de Castro, which leads diagonally from Largo do Pelourinho towards the ocean. The third bank is on the main business street, Rua J. G. Zarco. Open Monday to Friday from 8:30 am to 3 pm.

Camping: The campground is right on the beach, along Avenida Henrique towards Campo de Baixo. Follow the sign marked Praia down to the left. The large, sandy grounds offer almost no shade, since the palm trees are still rather small. A supermarket, snack bar with terrace, beach access, and play and television rooms are offered here. It is crowded in summer, especially during weekends and school holidays when many Madeirans make the trip over.

Car, Motorcycle, and Moped Rental: "Moinho," Rua Estevão de Alencastre, Porto Santo, Tel: 98 24 03 and "Atlantic," Avenida Vieira de Castro, Tel: 98 26 83. Motorcycles can also be rented at "Moinho" (Yamaha 80 for 4500$00 per day). Smaller motorbikes are rented at "Urs Moser Diving Center," Rua João Gonçalves Zarco 5 (almost on the beach, across from the market), Tel: 98 21 62, 3900$00 per day.

Medical Care: The hospital in Vila Baleira is at the east entrance to town on Rua Dr. José Diamantino Lima, Tel: 98 22 11.

Police: Travessa das Matas, Tel: 98 24 23.

Post Office: On Avenida Vieira de Castro, open Monday to Friday from 9 am to 12:30 pm and 2:30 to 5:30 pm.

Restaurants: There are several snack bars and restaurants, where the selection is not always large but is always tasty.

"Marques," near the bus stop, Rua João Santana, well-maintained, very good seafood reasonably priced. "Baiana" on Largo do Pelourinho is open almost all day; one can also order soup, sandes and tostas. "Arsénios" on the beach promenade, "Forno" on the way out of town to the west. As alternatives to the restaurants in Vila Baleira, try "Estrela do Norte" in Camacha and "Estrela da Calheta" in Calheta, both offer simple but delicious food.

Sports and Recreation: In terms of athletic activities, there is plenty to do even on this small island.

Cycling: There is a bicycle rental on Avenida Henrique, which goes from Vila Baleira to the west. The bicycles are rather old, so one should definitely check the brakes before setting out.

The route along the south coast is the least steep. If one rides along the other roads, one will have to get off and push now and then, but that makes the downhill sections even more enjoyable (if the brakes are in good shape). Cycling all the way around the island is quite an accomplishment, especially if strong winds are added to the challenges presented by steep hills and old bikes.

Bicycles cost 1000$00 a day to rent, but are also available by the hour with prices adjusted accordingly.

Horseback Riding: At the "Quinta dos Projetas" one can take riding lessons, or rent a horse and ride out alone or with a guide on the beach or all over the island. Prices per person and hour lie between 1300$00 and 2000$00, Tel: 98 31 65.

Swimming: The temperature of the ocean is such that swimming is possible almost all year (16 to 18 °C, 61 to 65 °F). The water is clear, the fine, sandy beach slopes gently into the sea, and if it is windy enough, the waves can get quite large. It is very important, however, to be an accurate judge of one's abilities as a swimmer, since many sections of the shore have no lifeguard.

At the hotel Porto Santo there is, of course, a swimming pool.

Scuba Diving: There is a Swiss-run diving school on the beach at Vila Baleira, which is open from April to November. Diving excursions are offered along the south coast. Contact "Urs Moser Diving Center," Tel: 98 21 62.

Hiking: The long beach is, naturally, a lovely place to walk. The best time is at ebb tide, when the sand is smooth and hard, and one can walk from Vila Baleira to the island's westernmost point.

Pico do Castello can be reached from Vila Baleira in an hour and 45 minutes. A shorter way is to take the bus to Camacha first. Several routes lead to the top of this conical mountain; just keep going uphill. At the summit is a monument to *Antonio Shiappa de Azevedo* and has an unlimited view of the whole island. From here to the peak to the east, *Pico do Facho,* the trail is strenuous.

On a hiking loop along the road from Vila Baleira to *Serra da Fora* over the *Serra de Dentro* and around both peaks, one gets to know the whole eastern part of the island and can make a side trip to *Fonte da Areira* to admire the north coast cliffs. Along the way, one encounters at least one of the windmills which are so characteristic of the island.

Tourist Information: Turismo (the tourist information office) is right across from the big pier; it is also accessible from the courthouse going onto Avenida Vieira de Castro. Here one finds free maps of the island, bus schedules, and tips for current events or especially nice walks (in English). Private rooms or holiday flats can be arranged here, too. The office is open Monday to Friday from 9 am to 12:30 pm and 2 to 5:30 pm, Tel: 98 23 61/2.

Transportation: Several busses run on the island, connecting small villages with Vila Baleira and it with the harbour, timed for departures and arrivals of the ferry. The bus schedule is available free of charge at Turismo. Ferries and flights go to Madeira.

→*Travel on Madeira*

Postal System

A letter or postcard to any EC nation costs 60$00. Mail between Europe and Madeira is sent by air and takes from 4 to 7 days, sometimes longer. After post office hours, postage stamps and telephone cards may also be purchased at some kiosks.

→*Business Hours, Telephone*

Prazeres

The name of this village, "pleasures," was allegedly given it on account of the exceptionally beautiful landscape surrounding it — and deservedly so. Otherwise, Prazeres is a rather unimpressive, sprawling village, though it does have *Miradouro,* or scenic viewpoint with signs pointing the way. For a view of the sea, one should follow the road past the junk shop towards the shore. Fields, vegetable gardens, and fruit trees characterise the village. There is a restaurant/bar at the small village plaza.

Quintas and Parks

Almost all estates (quintas) have a large ornamental garden. The first quintas were built in the 15th century, but the gardens were added much later at the end of the 18th century. For botanists and landscapers alike, they are a veritable treasure, due to the rich array of plants (some of which are quite old) and exemplary landscaping.

The former owners imported plants from all over the world, so today one sees a mixture from the most varied vegetation zones. Geometric designs, hedges,

The most diverse types of plants from every corner of the world thrive in the Quintas and parks

flower beds, arbours, fountains, greenhouses and ponds add diversity. Many of these historical gardens are definitely worth seeing and open to the public.

In addition, there are several parks, such as Monte's city park, the D. Amélia city garden or the Ribeiro Frio nature park, which are always open.

Here, only a few quintas are described, the rest are listed under the relevant individual entries. Orchid lovers should visit the *Quinta da Boa Vista*. One can visit the large orchid greenhouse and even purchase flowers or order them to take home. The quinta is on Rua L. F. Albuquerque in the eastern section of Funchal, Tel: 2 04 68. Hours: Monday to Saturday from 9 am to 5:30 pm.

In the garden at *Quinta Magnólia* on Rua Dr. Pita, there are many opportunities to get some exercise, for instance, a fitness course, tennis courts, swimming pool, etc. In the historic residence, formerly home of the British Country Club, one can have lunch or 5 o'clock tea in a cultivated atmosphere. Service is provided by students of the hotel management school. There is also an art exhibition here. The quinta is open daily from 8 am to 9 pm. The restaurant is open only during weekdays; lunch is served promptly at 1 pm and the bar opens at noon. Reservations are recommended, Tel: 6 40 13.

A popular destination for Madeirans: the neighbouring island of Porto Santo

The *Quinta Vigia,* workplace of the regional president, also has a garden from which one has a beautiful view of Funchal and the harbour.

Quinta das Cruzes →Funchal/Archeological Museum, Quinta do Bom Sucesso →Funchal/Botanical Garden, Quinta do Palheiro Ferreira →Funchal/Quintas, Gardens and Parks, Quinta do Governo →Santo da Serra, Quinta do Nossa Senhora da Conceição →Monte

Rabaçal

A winding, very narrow roadway leads from Paúl da Serra down into the valley of Rabaçal. Located among the heather-covered slopes of Paúl da Serra, Rabaçal has the ambiance of a friendly little oasis, whose lush Mediterranean vegetation stands in beautiful contrast to the seemingly monotonous slopes. There are inviting picnic spots at the Rabaçal forester's hut. With prior reservations and a permit, one can also stay the night at the forester's hut. Permits and reservations can be obtained at "Quinta Vigia" *(→Funchal/ Quintas).* The paths to Risco waterfall and the 25 Fontes (springs) are highly recommended and pass through beautiful countryside *(→Hiking).*

Religion

Madeira's population is predominantly Roman Catholic. Due to the centuries of British influence, there is a small Anglican congregation in Funchal which holds regular services. There is a small Scottish Protestant church on the west side of the city gardens, Rua do Conselheiro 48. Information on church services can be obtained at the hotel reception or tourist information office.

Restaurants

There is a multitude of restaurants in Funchal; from simple, local dishes which one can often watch being prepared, to a several-course meal at a five-star hotel, one can find just about everything. There are many exquisite seafood restaurants whose prices correspond to the quality of the food. Chinese, English, and Italian food are also available. Most restaurants, in addition to local specialties, also serve international cuisine. Prices are similar to those in central Europe and are higher than in Portugal, although it is certainly possible to find good meals consisting of soup and main course in a simple restaurant for 1000$00. Before every meal, bread and butter — pão e manteiga — are served automatically. Outside Funchal, restaurants will only be found in the larger towns; they will occasionally offer lunch for travellers, but no dinner. One can, of course, get a snack at a café or snack bar *(→Cuisine).*

Ribeira Brava

Ribeira Brava lies in a valley that opens onto the ocean and is surrounded on the other three sides by mountains. The road from Funchal winds down in serpentines, offering a lovely view over the village. At first glance, Ribeira Brava seems a quiet, dreamy little place. This impression is shattered when the busloads of tourists which stop here on their tour of the island swarm into town, populating the little shore promenade with its modest shopping centre, a few cafés, and the souvenir shops. Just at the entrance to town, there is a modern building which resembles a cement block; mildly put, it looks rather out of place among the old, traditional houses. It contains a supermarket, bank, and hotel, which document the attempt to move some tourism out of Funchal and into the smaller towns. In spite of this, Ribeira Brava has retained its own charm, making it worth a visit.

Ribeira Brava / **History**

The settlement of Ribeira Brava was founded in 1440, and the quickly growing population lived from sugar cane cultivation and agriculture. The river which gave the town its name, Ribeira Brava ("wild river"), often caused such extensive floods after rainfall that early residents were unable to cross the mountains to São Vicente on the northern side. Farmers living in villages along this route, such as Serra de Água, were often cut off for weeks from other towns. On the shore promenade, one can see the remains of a fort from the 18th century. The triangular *Forte do São Bento,* St. Benedict's fort, was built by the governor and captain general Duarte Sodré Pereira in 1708. It was destroyed in 1803 by one of Ribeira Brava's most severe floods.

Ribeira Brava / **Sights**

The ruins of the 18th century *Forte São Bento* on the shore promenade cannot be overlooked.

The village church, *São Bento,* with its blue and white tile roof is from the last half of the 15th century; it was, however, destroyed and rebuilt many times. The church construction, therefore, lacks any special architectural value. Inside, there is a baptismal font from the time of King D. Manuel (1385-1433), a pulpit from the 16th century, some paintings of Portuguese-Flemish origin from the 16th to 18th centuries, and goldsmith work.

The paving stones in the churchyard also deserve attention: the various ways in which they were laid create many different and designs according to viewing angle. At the church is the monument to Jesuit father Manuel Álvares (1526-1583), who wrote a standard work on Latin grammar·and lived in Ribeira Brava.

Ribeira Brava / **Practical Information**

Accommodation: Hotel "Brava Mar" at the entrance to town. Single room with breakfast: 5250$00, double room with breakfast, 7000$00, Tel: 95 22 20/4; Telex: 722 58 BAMAR P. These prices might be higher during the peak season.

Banks: One bank is located to the left of the church, on the same street as Centro de Saúde; the other is in the modern building at the entrance to town. These are open Monday to Friday from 8:30 am to 3 pm.

Festivals: The festival of *São Pedro* on June 29 is one that attracts young and old, tourists and Madeirans alike from all over the island. During the last several years, an amateur passion play has been performed by citizens of Ribeira Brava on the morning of Good Friday, featuring "original" costumes. In October, *Fest das Bandas* is celebrated, featuring performances by music groups from the region.

Medical Care: The Centro de Saúde is just to the left of the church.

Restaurants: The restaurant and snack bar "A Parada" are located right behind the church, next to the river. The restaurant is in the basement, and serves good, Madeiran food at normal prices. There are other (sidewalk) cafés directly along the shore.

The village church of Ribeira Brava was destroyed and rebuilt a number ot times

On the road to Ponta do Sol, the restaurant "Água Mar" is on the left. One can dine with a view of the sea, which costs somewhat more than at "A Parada." However, compared to central European prices, one can eat well and economically here.

Shopping: There is a supermarket, *Lidosol,* in the modern cement building at the entrance to town. Souvenir shops and a small shopping centre are located on the beach promenade, where a market also takes place.

Swimming: The beach at Ribeira Brava is rocky, and the road runs right along the shore. The conditions are therefore not ideally suited to swimming, but sunbathing is possible if one is not bothered by the stones.

Transportation: Busses 6, 7, 107. Funchal is 31 km (19 miles) away. The service station is located at the entrance to town.

Ribeiro Frio

Ribeiro Frio lies amid lush woods. The stream *Ribeiro Frio* is diverted through a beautifully constructed trout hatchery. A forestry station keeps watch over the fishery, and thanks to the crystal-clear water, one can observe the fish in all stages of their development. A log cabin houses "Victor's Bar," which serves excellent food, including trout ("Truta" in Portuguese).

A hiking trail along a shady levada leads from here to the overlook *Balcões* in about an hour.

Transportation: Bus no. 103 (towards Boaventura).

Santa Cruz

This town is heavily influenced by its proximity to the airport. The airport highway ER 101 bisects Santa Cruz, a town founded in 1450. It offers several restaurants, accommodation, a city park, a shopping centre, a market hall, and a beach. The beach is 200 to 300 metres (650 to 980 feet) long, and stony; a small swimming pool serves as an alternative to rough Atlantic waves. While swimming, one can watch (and unfortunately also hear) the planes take off and land. The church at Santa Cruz is from the first half of the 16th century; its architectural style is Gothic-Manueline. It possesses three naves, which is unusual for Madeira, a Spanish-Moorish ceiling, and azulejos, the painted wall tiles.

Santa Cruz / **Practical Information**

Accommodation: "Pensão Matos," across from the market hall, only Portuguese is spoken, simple, prices for double occupancy vary with the season and the owner's mood (2500$00 to 4000$00).

The residencial "A Varanda" (with restaurant), Tel: 5 21 18, lies in *Santa Catalina* directly above the airport. Its location makes it ideal for travellers who depart early in the morning or arrive late at night and have not yet made reservations. If coming from Funchal on ER 101, turn left towards Santo da Serra, or turn right if coming from the airport.

Banks: Seen from the beach, there is a bank behind the church.

Medical Care: The Centro de Saúde is behind the small city park near the beach.

Restaurants: There is a small café at the shopping centre. At the "Pombalhal" restaurant at city park, one should definitely try the *sopa de tomate e cebola,* the tomato and onion soup. For lighter appetites, it is a sufficient main dish and is inexpensive as well. The restaurant is at the back of the house, the café is at the front. Yet another economically priced restaurant, "O Tubo," is located diagonally across from the supermarket (behind the churchyard to the left and on to the small village square). More cafés are located around the market hall. One can dine in Santa Catarina with a view of the airplanes *(→Accommodation).*

Shopping: There is a small, modest shopping centre on the other side of ER 101. The Supermercado Santa Cruz can be found by going to the left behind the church. The market hall is open weekdays until noon.

Santana

This picturesque little town in the northeast of Madeira — whose colourful straw-roofed houses appear in countless books and brochures as characteristic of the island — was founded at the end of the 16th century. The name comes from the town's patron saint, St. Anna or Sant'Ana as she is called in Portuguese. The 17th century church is dedicated to her.

Santana's houses

The wooden houses with straw roofs closely resemble those first built on Madeira by the original settlers, since wood and straw were abundant at that time. There are three basic types of house. The simplest has one rectangular room and a straw-covered saddle roof, the edges of which nearly touch the ground ("casa de empena de fio"). The "casas do sobrado" differ from these in that they have an attic with a small skylight where tools are usually kept. The third type, "casas de quatro águas," is normally built of stone, and the straw roof does not reach as far down as is typical of the first type. These are, as a rule, larger than both kinds of wooden houses. The floor space is often divided into two rooms by a wooden wall, and the kitchen is in a separate extension.

The exposed wooden slats are brightly painted, and every year, the most beautiful house is awarded a prize.

Many of these traditional houses are still occupied, but one often sees corrugated tin roofs instead of the labour-intensive and expensive straw, which must be replaced every four years. The lack of comfort and roominess understandably induces owners to built a modern dwelling next to the quaint but truly uncomfortable cottages of their grandparents. The city of Santana is aware of this trend and of the touristic value of the "Santana houses." Therefore, the city gives house owners financial support and try to impress upon them the importance of maintaining their houses.

A few prime examples have been maintained as tourist attractions (take the street across from the church up to the left; the town centre is also here).

Santana / **Practical Information**

General: Located at the centre of town are the post office, bus stop, taxi stand, pharmacy, bar, restaurant and guest house. The "exemplary" houses are here, as well. To reach the centre, take the street across from the church leading up to the left.

Accommodation: The only guest house belongs to the restaurant: "O Colmo," 16 rooms, double occupancy 5000$00, reservations recommended.

Banks: The bank is located in a rather tasteless cement imitation of a Santana house, diagonally across from the church towards São Jorge.

Festivals: In July, *24 Horas a Bailar* is celebrated, where singing and dancing continue for 24 hours. Folklore groups, local bands and singers make up a diverse programme that actually does last 24 hours from one late afternoon to the next. The *Festa do Compadres* takes place shortly before Mardi Gras. The *compadre* - godfather — and the *comadre* - godmother — are represented as straw dolls that are constantly fighting. In plays and parades, the dolls are presented to the public. The festival's high point is when the dolls are burned.

Restaurants: There is one restaurant in Santana, which of course does great business and whose owner is, in terms of prices, aware of his monopoly. "O Colmo" ("roofing straw"), near the courthouse and the Santana houses. Tel: 57 24 78, 57 31 24.

Transportation: Bus no. 103.

Santo da Serra

Santo da Serra lies 660 metres (around 2,200 feet) above sea level and northeast of Santa Cruz. On the one hand, it seems to be a quiet, untouched village, but on the other, one cannot help but notice the busy construction going on all around and the villas nearby. However, the centre of the village has retained its charm thanks to the small shops, cafés and restaurants located at the plaza in front of the church. If the church is open, one should have a look at the tower from inside because the windows have lovely and various colours which create interesting light effects which change with the position of the sun. The *Quinta do Santo* is on the road to Santa Cruz. One enters the garden through a wrought-iron gate to find beautiful, azalea-lined paths and many camelias, hortensias, magnolias, and old, lichen-covered trees that give the park and quinta buildings a timeless feeling. Further inside, one encounters a somewhat desolate game enclosure and a few ponies. The star of the menagerie is a small kangaroo. The garden also contains a tennis court, miniature golf course, and a number of picnic sites. Santo da Serra is the trailhead for the hike along *Levada da Serra* to Camacha.

Santo da Serra / **Practical Information**

Festivals: In June, there is a festival in honour of St. Anthony (inquire at Turismo about the exact date).

Medical Care: Coming from Machico, the Centro de Saúde is at the entrance to town.

Shopping: At the village square and behind the church are shops, cafés, and a supermarket.

Sports and Recreation: The golf course lies a bit out of town along the road to Santa Cruz (→*Sports and Recreation*). From here, one can walk to Camacha, Portela or to Levada do Furado towards Ribeiro Frio.

Transportation: From Funchal, one can take bus no. 77 via Camacha, or numbers 20 or 25 via Santa Cruz.

São Jorge

São Jorge and its neighbouring village Arco de São Jorge are agricultural settlements; the land surrounding them is very fertile. Wine grapes and willows are

The symbol of a past era — the classic Santana houses

the primary crops. The bundled willow twigs often line the roads making for a picturesque scene. Along ER 101 between Arco de São Jorge and São Jorge, one should stop often to enjoy the truly beautiful landscape. There are many nice views of the Atlantic. The valleys are deep green and highly terraced. Tree ferns, eucalyptus, pines, and laurels are covered with ivy, giving this region a very lush appearance. The waterfalls are a beautiful natural attraction that can be seen from the road.

São Vicente

São Vicente is most quickly and easily reached over the pass via ER 104, which goes through *Encumeada*. After crossing Encumeada pass with its sparse alpine vegetation, the voluptuous green valley of São Vicente seems like an oasis.

The town lies right on the coast and is enclosed by densely wooded foothills. Scattered palms create a vaguely Mediterranean mood. São Vicente is an enchanting little village. However it is impossible to drive a car in the centre of this town because the streets are so narrow. Thus, it possesses a delightfully peaceful atmosphere, soon to be disturbed by the attempt to shift some tourism from Funchal to other towns. "Progress," of course, does not stop for little jewels like São Vicente. In the near future, two additional hotels and restaurants will be completed.

The little chapel by the sea is worth viewing; it is built into a cliff. A trip along ER 101 leads through some very lovely country; the road itself winds along the coastal cliffs in a fashion which could almost be called artistic. Towards Porto Moniz there are a number of waterfalls plunging dramatically from the clifftops.

From São Vicente, one can go on hikes to Encumeada, or visit a lava grotto. A guide is necessary, since the grotto and the way into it are hard to find. Information is available at hotel "Estalagem do Mar" (→*Accommodation*) or at the city administration at the courthouse ("Câmara Municipal," large, new building near the church).

São Vicente / **Practical Information**

Accommodation: As of 1991, there was only one hotel in São Vicente: the exclusive "Estalagem do Mar" has a restaurant, double occupancy from 6500$00, single rooms from 5000$00, suites for 10,000$00, a squash court, miniature golf, video arcade, and sauna. Tel: 84 26 15, Fax: 8 42 77 65, 9240 S. Vicente. As of 1991, another hotel is under construction.

Banks and Pharmacy: Two banks and a pharmacy are in the immediate vicinity of the village church, S. Vicente.

Festivals: "Festa de São Vicente" on January 22, "Festa da Nossa Senhora do Rosário" on the first Sunday in October.

Post Office: There is a "credifone" booth and post office on the same street as the restaurant "Pub O Corvo." This is open from 9 am to 12:30 pm and 2:30 to 6 pm (→*Restaurants*).

Restaurants: "Pub O Corvo" restaurant is located in the centre of town; it is a bar and café as well. It has a more modern design and is not typically Portuguese. To find it, go diagonally behind the church and turn left into the street by the "Mercearia Alealdade," a variety store; "Pub O Corvo" is about a 20 minute walk along here.

On the road to Seixal, there are two other restaurants right on the coast: "Quebra Mar" in an ugly, tasteless, confusing new building which at least has a view of the ocean; and a smaller, more "typical" and less fancy restaurant is on the left side toward Seixal. There are also 3 other bars/cafés, and an additional restaurant is being built.

Seixal

If one does not stop in Seixal, one might not notice that there is a village here. The village is spread out along ER 101, and the tiny centre of town beyond the road has a small harbour. The natural swimming pool is the main attraction in Seixal and is worth a visit. From the street with the small bars and restaurants, one follows the sign marked "Piscina" through some small gardens and finds the steep footpath to the pools. The natural rock formations form pools of various sizes and depths, whose edges have to some extent been stabilised with cement. The "Café Arco-Íris," where one can inquire about private rooms, is also on this road.

The residents of Seixal make their living primarily from agriculture and the cultivation of grapevines. The fields are protected from the harsh north wind by *urze,* the dried branches of heather.

Sights

Madeira's imposing landscape and lush vegetation are probably the island's most outstanding characteristics. The rugged coastline, lush valleys with waterfalls, lofty peaks (over 1,800 metres/5,900 feet), Funchal's peaceful bay, and the heavenly sandy beach on the neighbouring island of Porto Santo, are examples of the geographic variety and natural beauty found here. The cultivated landscape is equally interesting and full of special features: terracing, irrigation, animal husbandry, tropical and subtropical crops, and tropical decorative plants in the artistically laid out gardens from the 18th and 19th centuries. Madeira's greatest claim to fame is its wine, whose tradition and production are demonstrated at many wineries. Agricultural products, fish (especially deep-sea fish and tuna) exotic fruits, and flowers (especially orchids and strelitzias) are sold at the colourful and lively daily markets.

There are museums (mostly in Funchal) covering every topic and historical period in Madeiran history, including the present.

Especially outstanding architectural masterpieces are not present on the island. Many churches, monasteries and convents were built at the time of settlement, many are Manueline, and nearly all were influenced by the Baroque. The traditional dwellings of rural Madeirans are unique, tiny, primitive, and now usually stand empty. The country estates, or quintas, show the early influence of the British elite during the past century.

Once a year, at New Year's Eve, is an impressive fireworks display, and visitors from all over the world flock to Funchal to admire the show. Around the New Year, Funchal is especially exciting and vibrant since many cruise ships stop here at this time.

Speed Limits

In towns and villages, 60 km/h (36 mph) is the maximum speed allowed, and on local motorways it is 90 km/h (54 mph), unless otherwise posted. Road conditions and the amount of traffic usually only allow for speeds between 30 and 50 km/h (18 to 30 mph).

Sports and Recreation

Most athletic activities are concentrated in Funchal, and there is a lot to choose from. Most of the larger hotels have swimming pools or direct access to the ocean, tennis and squash courts, fitness rooms, miniature golf, sailing, and windsurfing. There are many opportunities to engage in sports on one's own as well.

Fishing: At Funchal's harbour are several companies offering deep-sea fishing excursions. The trips last 3 to 7 hours, and all equipment is provided. Beginners receive instruction (in English). A seven-hour excursion costs around 21,250$00. However, in light of the fact that people concerned with preserving nature try to get laws passed to protect the waters surrounding Madeira and the Desertas, it is amazing that sport fishing — sometimes for endangered species — is still allowed!

Golf: The golf course at Santo da Serra occupies one of Madeira's few large, flat pieces of land. It is located 25 km (15 miles) from Funchal or 3 km (almost 2 miles) from the airport. In 1991, the course was expanded to 27 holes. Information is available at the following address: Quinta do Lago da Madeira, Santo Antonio da Serra, 9100 Santa Cruz, Tel: 5 53 45, Telex: 7 26 70, Olagom P.

Hiking: →Hiking

Horseback Riding: A private riding club lies outside Funchal on E 201 toward Camacha. Riding lessons and horse rentals can be booked in Funchal at the hotels "Mimosa," Tel: 3 26 58 or "Estrelícia," Tel: 3 01 31.

On Porto Santo, one can ride on the beach (→Porto Santo).

Swimming: In Funchal, there are swimming pools at Quinta Magnólia (135$00) and Lido (200$00) in addition to the hotel pools, some of which also have direct access to the sea. The Lido is a spacious, popular place with ocean access and other water sports, such as surfing, water-skiing and paddle boats. Additionally, the "Club Naval do Funchal" and "Club de Turismo da Madeira," both on the Estrada Monumental in the hotel district, offer assorted water sports. The natural swimming pools at Porto Moniz and Seixal have, of course, a totally different atmosphere from the hotel pools. They are open from July to October, and admissions costs only 60$00.

The Lido Galomar is a public pool in Caniço de Baixo, and Santa Cruz also has a small swimming pool on the sea.

Scuba Diving: An enthusiastic German diver has a scuba school based in Funchal at the hotel "Madeira Carlton" and in Caniço de Baixo at the hotel "Galomar." One can take a certification course (with exam), or if one is already certified, just go diving. In either case, one needs a doctor's written permission; equipment can be rented. Diving excursions begin either right from shore, or from a boat for underwater destinations farther away. Since the underwater national park was founded, there is once more much to see and experience. The animals have had a chance to recover and repopulate in the strictly protected areas. Ask for information at the Hotel Madeira Carlton, Tel: 3 10 31 or from Rainer Waschkewitz himself, Tel: 93 20 10.

Porto Santo also has a diving school *(→Porto Santo)*.

Tennis: Quinta Magnólia's two tennis courts are open to the public. An hour costs only 135$00. For non-guests, the hotel courts are expensive.

Telephone

There are both coin and card operated telephones on Madeira.

Coin phones take 10$00, 20$00, and 50$00. It is often difficult to call overseas on them, not to mention the fact that the coins get eaten up faster than one can speak. Card operated phones are easier to use: one buys a "cartão de credifone" (a telephone card) picks up the receiver, and inserts the card in the slot. The dial tone can be heard immediately. There are two different phone cards: one for 750$00 with 50 units, and one for 1725$00 with 120 units (includes 5 free units). One unit lasts 3.5 seconds and costs 15$00. There are no times during the day when rates are reduced.

In Funchal at the post office on Avenida de Zarco *(→Funchal/Post Office)*, one can use a phone from 8:30 am to 10 pm.

In bars, guest houses, hotels, and cafés, units are usually at least twice as expensive as at the post office or in public phone booths.

For international calls, one must first dial the country code, then local or area code (if applicable, without the first zero), then the phone number.

When calling between Madeira and Portugal, one dials only the local or area code and the phone number.

Theatre

The large, beautiful building of the city theatre, or *Teatro Municipal,* is on Avenida Arriaga across from the city garden. Theatre troupes from the mainland give an occasional performance, or the Madeiran Ensemble puts on a play. Exhibitions and concerts are held here, and a cinema shows fairly current films. The schedule of performances can be had from Turismo or the daily paper.

Time of Day

Madeira, like Portugal, is on Greenwich Mean Time. This is one hour earlier than Central European time and 5 (New York) to 8 (Los Angeles) hours later than in the Continental United States. This is also true in summer.

Tourism

Ever since the 18th century, Madeira has been a travel destination of foreign visitors. At that time, this Atlantic island was mainly visited by the ill because of the mild

Its coulors are the same as the flag of Madeira, and the strelitzia was even declared the official flower of the island

climate. This was especially true for those suffering from tuberculosis. At the beginning of the 20th century, an exclusive spa-tourism was in vogue, which predominantly brought wealthy English to Madeira. European high society gathered mostly in Monte. There are many exclusive, posh hotels from this era, for instance, the well-known "Reid's Hotel," the "Savoy," and the "Grand Hotel Belmonte"; the latter is no longer used as a hotel, but instead houses a private school run by priests. Beginning in 1881, there were regular ocean voyages from England to Funchal, and after 1885 from Hamburg and Antwerp as well. Cruise ships have always stopped in Funchal. After Gago Coutinho landed a seaplane for the first time in Funchal harbour in 1921, regular seaplane flights to and from England began. These were stopped a short time later after a tragic accident. Only after the airport was completed in 1964 did the island become interesting for the greater public, since until that point, Madeira could only be reached by ship; planes had to land at the NATO base on Porto Santo. The holiday centre Matur came into being in the 1960's, built on what were vacant fields near Machino up to that point. The mild climate during the entire year attracts many older people fleeing the cold temperatures in central and northern Europe.

Tourism here is high-class and exclusive. The absence of large beaches and the rough terrain make it less interesting for the masses. Prices are clearly higher than in Portugal itself, since almost all goods must be imported. There are few economically-priced accommodations, and because of lack of space, there is only one campground. The geographic parameters drastically limit the construction of huge hotel complexes — there is simply not enough room.

All tourist facilities and attractions are concentrated in Funchal and a few other places on the southern coast, such as Caniço de Baixo and Machico. The capacities of this area are almost exhausted. Recently, hotels and restaurants have been built in the "backwoods" neglected by tourists. The island is ideal, however, for active and adventurous tourists. Madeira is a superb place for water sports and hiking.

The sand beach is Porto Santo's capital, which makes the otherwise quiet, sleepy island attractive to many in summer. Here, too, the hotel capacity is being expanded, which will hopefully not have a negative effect.

Traditionally, most tourists have come from England, followed by Germany, Scandinavia, and mainland Portugal.

Tourist Information

Information on Madeira can be obtained from tourist offices and travel agencies in one's home country.

In Great Britain: Portuguese National Tourist Office, Newbond St. House, 1/5 Newbond Street, London W1Y 0NP, Tel: 49 33 873.

In the United States: Portuguese National Tourist Office, 590 5th Avenue, New York, NY 10036-4704, Tel: 354-4403.

In Portugal, information is available from:

Direcção Geral do Turismo, Avenida António Augusto de Aguiar 86, 1200 Lisboa, Tel: 57 50 91.

The tourist office on Madeira has its headquarters in Funchal: Secretaria Regional do Turismo e Cultura, Av. Arriaga 18, 9000 Funchal, Tel: 2 90 57, Telex 7 21 41. At "Turismo," likewise at Avenida Arriaga 18, Tel: 2 56 58, maps, books and information in English are available. The office is open Monday to Saturday from 9 am to 8 pm; Sunday, from 9 am to 6 pm.

There are also tourist information offices in Câmara de Lobos, at the airport, in Machico, and on Porto Santo.

Traffic Regulations

In Portugal, one drives on the right, at intersections it's right before left unless otherwise posted. Traffic signs correspond to the international norms. Legal blood alcohol level is 0.5 (50 mills). Outside of towns and villages, wearing seat belts is mandatory, and children under 12 must sit in the back seat (→*Speed Limits*). The driving style on Madeira is typical of southern European countries: somewhat more emotional and actually too fast for the road conditions. They drive at maximum speeds in spite of challenging roads (60 km/h can be a breakneck speed on hairpin curves!). Honking the horn before every blind curve and in narrow streets is common practise and a good idea. Occasionally, one is forced to back up several hundred metres if the road is too narrow for two-way traffic. Traffic is Funchal is heavy and, due to the construction sites, quite chaotic. During rush hour (8 to 9 am and 5 to 7 pm), the streets look full to bursting as Madeirans commute to and from work.

Travel Documents

Documents required upon entering Portugal:

A valid passport (no visa is required for visits up to 2 months). Children under 16 must be registered in their parent's passport or have children's identification. Drivers: Driver's licence, automobile papers and proof of insurance.

For pets: A current, multilingual veterinary certificate of good health and proof of rabies vaccination (the vaccination must have been administered at least one month prior and at the most 12 months prior to entry).

Travel on Madeira

By Car

Road conditions do not meet European standards. Due to Madeira's topography, the roads are winding and narrow. In spite of short distances, one should allow plenty of time since one will usually have to drive slowly. →*Car Rental, Speed Limits*

By Bus

All towns and villages are generally easily accessible by bus, even if the schedule is tailored to the needs of Madeira's working population (very early departures in the morning and evening). Tickets are inexpensive. In the capital, Funchal, one can travel longer distances almost any time on the orange municipal buses. Information on bus schedules and routes in map form can be purchased at Turismo in Funchal for 100$00. This also includes the times and routes of the regional red-grey or green-grey buses. The main bus station is next to and behind the electricity plant at the east end of Avenida do Mar. One further stop for busses travelling west is across from the Hotel Carlton. One can buy tickets on the bus. Every bus ride on these narrow, winding roads is an adventure, and one learns to appreciate the skill of the drivers, who drive with confidence on steep roads and manoeuvre past larger vehicles and other buses with only a few centimetres to spare.
In addition to public buses, there are many different bus excursions and tours offered by travel agencies *(→Excursions)*.

By Ship

Ferries commute only between Funchal and Porto Santo. A catamaran leaves Funchal daily, except Tuesday, at 8 am for Porto Santo and returns at 5 pm (till the end of March) or at 6 pm (from April 1). Tickets are available at the ferry office at the yacht harbour (open Monday to Friday from 9 am to 1 pm and 2:30 to 5 pm) or at a travel agency. A one-day round-trip ticket costs 6400$00, with the return trip on a different day the price is 5200$00. If the wind is strong and the sea rough, the ferry does not run; the 2½ hour crossing can be quite strenuous if the water is rough. Medication for seasickness can help avoid what might otherwise be an unpleasant situation *(→Excursions)*.

By Taxi

Taxi stands are located at the larger plazas in all towns. There is no central telephone number for taxis since the drivers work for various small companies. Yellow taxis have meters and one can see a price list upon request *(→Excursions)*.

By Airplane

Madeira's airport is near Santa Cruz, about 23 km (about 14 miles) from Funchal. The short landing strip (1,800 metres/5,886 feet) will be lengthened in the near future by building out into the ocean on pillars. There are flights to the Azores, the Portuguese mainland, Porto Santo, and the usual European airports *(→Travelling to Madeira)*. A very small, 18-passenger TAP plane commutes several times a day (depending on season) to Porto Santo and back. The one-way trip costs 5400$00 *(→Excursions)*.

Travelling to Madeira

Madeira is about an hour's flight from the Azores or an hour and a half from Lisbon. Passenger ships are no longer in operation; only as part of a cruise is it possible to dock on Madeira.

Aside from package tours in all price ranges, charter flights are unquestionalbly the least expensive way of getting to Madeira. Seasonal price differences are minimal, since Madeira is a favourite holiday spot all year. During European school holidays and for celebrations such as Easter, Christmas, and New Year, flights are somewhat more expensive (roughly £30 or $50) than at other times.

Charter flights should be booked a few months ahead of time since it will be difficult to get seats one or two months prior to departure, especially if one travels at Easter or the New Year.

Standard flights are more expensive, and depending on the airline, one usually has to change planes in Lisbon, Porto, or Paris.

Inexpensive flights from Amsterdam or Brussels hardly make a difference, given the distance most travellers have to cover to reach Madeira.

It is possible to combine a trip to Madeira with stops in Lisbon, Porto, or the Azores. Charters and package tours are available.

The airport on Madeira is 23 km (14 miles) east of Funchal, near the village of Santa Cruz. During the day, busses 23 and 113 run to Funchal. From the airport to Funchal by taxi costs about 3000$00.

Vegetation

The vegetation of the island is extremely interesting, because an ancient plant culture still exists here, the lauraceous or laurel forest. This dense evergreen forest must have completely covered the island at the time of its discovery; it is not without reason that the island is called *Madeira,* meaning wood. Of the original forest, only small areas remain. Most of the forest was cut for lumber or cleared and burned for agriculture *(→Fruits, Agriculture).* Exotic plants were brought by seafarers making stopovers on Madeira, or by well-travelled and wealthy English. A diverse flora developed, composed of species found here and nowhere else in the world (endemics) and species that are native to Australia, Asia, Africa, and South and Central America. Because of the highly varied topography and climatic zones *(→Climate),* specific plant associations or societies and cultivated plant zones developed.

Botanists consider the **laurel woods** are considered to be remnants from the Tertiary Period. Before the Ice Age, Europe's climate was much milder than today, and laurel forests covered much of central and northern Europe. Thus, one can think of Madeira's forests as a living museum, whose 10,000 hectares (25,000 acres) are now protected. Today, the largest forests can be found near Ribeiro Frio (towards Santo da Serra), along the Ribeira da Janela (going from Rabaçal), and around the Caldeirão Verde (from Queimadas), where they have remained untouched.

Most laurel trees can be recognised by their tough, usually oval, dark green leaves, which they shed at different times of year (not according to season). The most important species are the Madeira laurel (Persea indica, *Vinhático),* which has very beautiful, reddish wood similar to mahogany, the foetid laurel (Ocotea foetens, *Til),* which can reach heights of 30 metres (98 feet); the Canary laurel (Laurus azorica); the wax myrtle (Myrrica faya); and the mayflower tree (Clethra arborea). The ericaceous shrubs such as Erica arborea (*Urze*) and Vaccinium madeirense (Madeira blueberry or *Uveira da Serra*) bring light colours into the botanical palette. There are many other species, for instance, **juniper** (Juniperus oxycedrus), whose wood is very dark and was used to create the lovely wooden ceilings in Funchal's cathedral, and **Sideroxylon marmulano,** whose wood is extremely hard and was used for ship building. The moist climate allows lichens, mosses, and ferns to thrive not only on the ground but also on the trees themselves, creating an atmosphere typical of ancient, tropical and subtropical forests.

Because the island is isolated, species have developed here which are found only on Madeira or have spread only as far as the other Atlantic islands. Included in this category of **endemics** are mainly herbaceous and shrubby plants, such as *Madeira Stork's Bill* (Geranium madeirense), *Echinum nervosum,* the *Madeira daisy* (Atgyranthemum pinnatidium), members of the euphorb family (Euphorbia piscatoria and mellifera), and members of a family that exists only on Madeira: Musschia aurea and M. wollastonii. The presence of endemic **orchids** is especially interesting from a botanical point of view, though individual specimens look rather modest compared to cultivated orchids. If one looks carefully, one with find them off the beaten track in shady places. When walking in rocky terrain or along cliffs near the picos, sooner or later one will see impressive specimens of the *glandular aeonium* (Aeonium glandulosum), whose flat, round forms press up against the rocks and often have diameters of up to 40 cm (16 inches). The sticky aeonium (Aeonium glutinosum) is also in this family and can be found in drier regions.

In addition to the laurel woods, there are extensive **pine and eucalyptus forests,** which are used commercially. Firewood and good quality lumber are obtained from different species of acacia, which are also known as mimosa. In the early months of the year, they brighten up the forests with their numerous and intense yellow blossoms.

Middle European trees such as **oak, beech,** and *sycamore* are also found here. High elevations are exposed to extreme weather conditions (less moisture, more intense sunlight, stronger wind). **Heather and shrubs** thrive here, but have suffered under the grazing of sheep and goats. In these plant associations, one finds *Madeira blueberry,* Madeiran *elderberry and barberry, Madeiran saxifrage* (Saxifraga madeirensis), *hen-and-chicks, grasses,* and *ferns,* predominantly the *eagle fern.*

The most common **succulents** include the *prickly-pear cactus* (Opuntia tuna) and the *American agave* (Agave americana), which astoundingly thrive on cliffs and steep slopes.

The **palms** and **exotic ornamentals** characterise the vegetation of the southern coast. The size and stature of these plants never ceases to amaze.

The **Canary date palm** (Phoenix canariensis) cannot be overlooked, though it seldom reaches its potential height of 15 metres (50 feet) on Madeira. The crowns have compound leaves 5 to 6 metres long (16 to 20 feet) and bushy fruit clusters. The stately palms can be seen along avenues and boulevards, for instance, along the avenue in front of the quay on Porto Santo. Unfortunately, the dates are inedible. The king's palm from Cuba is also frequently planted along avenues.

Tree ferns (huge variations of ferns, having woody trunks and large, feathery leaves) and agaves including the famous *yucca* should not be mistaken for palms. **Dragon trees** (Dracena drago) occur only on Madeira, the Canary Islands, and Cape Verde, and likewise belong to the agave family. It is easy to spot the imposing, ancient specimens found here. The smooth, highly branched trunk, with bunches of sword-shaped leaves at the tips, possesses the botanical anomaly (for this group of plants) of increasing in circumference after vertical growth has ceased, quite the opposite of palms.

Exotic trees and shrubs are obvious due to their colourful blossoms. The Argentinian *Jacaranda* blooms from April to May, and has lilac or violet blossoms. Jacarandas line the Avenida Arriage in Funchal. In the garden at Quinta Vigia is a very large *African tulip tree,* which brings forth red flowers in autumn. *Callistemon* (bottle brush) also has red blossoms and is easily recognised by its characteristic inflorescence. The *Frangipani* bears its flowers and leaves at the ends of thick, evenly branched twigs, and the *sausage tree* has fruits needing no further explanation. *Hortensias, agapanthus, African love flower, and klivias* flourish almost everywhere. One can enjoy the sight of *poinsettia* and *hibiscus* in gardens and parks. Favourite climbers are *bouganvillaea* and *glyzinas.*

Calla lilies grow everywhere, among willow plantations, gardens, and even on compost piles. *Anthurium* is a little fussier, but still common in gardens, as are *orchids,* which are common in pots on terraces. At the end of this incomplete list, let the perhaps most well-known and beloved plant make its appearance: the *Strelitzia,* named after Charlotte von Mecklenburg-Strelitz and is closely related to the banana. The orange strelitzia comes from South Africa, and its blossoms resemble the head of a bird of paradise. The white strelitzia bears a similar, though larger, white blossom on a black-violett bract. The blue-yellow colour of the strelitzia is identical to Madeira's flag, and was thus made the official flower a few years ago.

Further descriptions →*Fruit, Agriculture, Travel Literature*

Vinháticos

The state-run hotel *Pousada dos Vinháticos* is housed in a rustic but nice building made of basalt.

Thanks to its convenient location on ER 104 between Ribeira Brava and São Vicente, the Pousada (founded in 1929) is a favourite place to stay for hikers who want to use this as a base to explore the surrounding mountains. The 15 rooms with a mountain view are usually always booked, making reservations mandatory (double occupancy 8000$00/single room 6700$00). Reservations can be made through a travel agency or the Hotel Estrelícia in Funchal *(→Funchal/Accomodations)*. If in doubt, one can contact the Turismo in Funchal.

A small restaurant with average prices, rustic atmosphere, and a fireplace is open daily. Reservations are recommended.

Pousada dos Vinháticos, Serra de Água, Tel: 95 23 44.

The houses in the small village of **Serra de Água** cannot be reached by car. The road ends at a hydroelectric plant fed by mountain rivers. The drainage pipe, visible from as far away as Ribeira Brava, also ends here.

Transportation: Bus no. 6 (towards Boaventura) runs three times a day, travel time about 2 hours.

Weather

Current weather reports from the meteorological station in Funchal are posted in Turismo and in most hotels. It is very important to check them before starting out on a hike.

→Climate, Hiking

Weights and Measures

Portugal uses the metric system including degrees Celsius.

Wine

The word "wine" on Madeira does not mean table wine, it means *Madeira*. In Portuguese, the word Madeira means three different things. First, it can simply mean "wood." Second, the Atlantic archipelago was given this name by virtue of the dense forests covering the island. Third, it means the liqueur wine, typical of the island and produced only here. Alcohol content ranges from 18 to 20%.

Wine / **An introduction to viniculture**

Four grape types have come to dominate viniculture here, whose names also indicate the taste of the wine.

Malvasier or Malmsey, as the English say, is the sweetest Madeira. It is dark, has a full-bodied flavour and strong bouquet, and is served with desserts or as an aperitif. Malmsey was the most well-known and beloved Madeira wine in England. The grapes were brought to the island in the 15th century from Crete.

Boal or Bual is the semi-sweet, mild Madeira with a light bouquet. Boal is served with dessert. The grape originally came from Burgundy.

Verdelho is the semidry Madeira. It is excellently suited to soups or as an aperitif. The grape, as in the case of Boal and Sercial, was brought by Jesuits to Madeira around 1600.

Sercial is the driest Madeira wine. Amber coloured, light, and very aromatic, Sercial was prized as an aperitif on many historical occasions, for instance, after the first flight over the English Channel in 1907. The Sercial grape is related to the German Riesling.

Tinta Negra Mole is a less refined grape variety, which is used as the basis for most of the Madeira wines (a blending grape).

Additional grape types, which have little importance today because they were almost completely eliminated by the grape-louse plague, are *Terrantez, Bastardo,* and *Carão de Moça.*

The four types (Sercial, Boal, Verdelho, Malvasier) are usually three years old when they are put on the market. The wines are blended, that is, they receive the taste typical of the winery by being mixed with other varieties, above all with Tinta Negro Mole. Prices correspond to age and brand of the wine. Young Madeira wines are sold from 700$00 per bottle.

Vintage is the name applied to wines made from the first-class grapes of a particular year, and have been aged at least 20 years in casks. The youngest vintage wines on the market are at least 25 years old, because it takes about a quarter of a century including the aging process (in the cask and in the bottle) and quality control to produce a vintage wine. Vintage wines are of superior quality, which they retain even after 100 years. A 40-year-old vintage costs between 9000$00 and 10,000$00, a 60-year-old may cost upwards of 15,000$00. There are even vintages dating from before the grape-louse catastrophe in 1873!

Solera are wines from first-class grapes — like the vintages — that age slowly in barrels. In contrast to the vintages, a Solera is continually extended with younger wine of the same quality as soon as a certain volume has evaporated in the aging process. The vintner chooses the Solera method when he does not have enough wine of a particular year to make a vintage. Soleras are thus obviously less expensive than vintages. A bottle of Solera from 1898 can be bought starting at 8000$00.

Vinho de canteiro is the wine warmed only by the sun shining on closed casks, no artificial heat source is employed. This traditional, very lengthy and expensive method of wine making is used today only by the winery *Artur de Barros e Sousa* on Madeira.

The quality grade **finest** is given to blended wines whose youngest component is 3 years old.

Reserve and **special reserve** are terms applied to wines that are at least 5 or 10 years old, respectively.

The typical **wine glass** has a short stem, is rounded at the bottom and narrows toward the top. Madeira wines can be stored indefinitely in an upright position and do not need to be cooled. An open bottle of Madeira will also keep a long time without oxidising.

The date on blended wines, that is, on all wines except vintages, is that of the youngest wine added.

Madeira is also used in sauces, fish, meat, and poultry dishes. These wines are made mostly of the *Tinta Negra Mole* grape.

Wine / **History**

As early as the middle of the 15th century, Prince Dom Henrique O Navegador had grapevines brought to Madeira from Crete. The grapes had ideal growing conditions on the Atlantic island. An average yearly temperature of 20 °C (68 °F), a mild sunny climate, and mineral and nitrogen-rich volcanic soil let the grapes thrive. Wine was, in comparison to sugar cane, not a very important product in the early colonial years. Only after the sugar cane business declined *(→History)* and the Azores established themselves as grain supplier to mainland Portugal did vineyards increase and wine become a significant trading commodity.

The wine (which, up to that time had "only" distinguished itself among other European wines due to its special quality but was not yet "Madeira" in the current sense) was exported to many European countries and especially to the England, the main importer of wine from Madeira.

This wine was so popular there that the kingdom also had it exported to its overseas colonies. The Madeira wine was the only non-English product England allowed to be shipped directly to the new colonies; according to 17th century English law, everything else had to be sent via England. Two historical facts are always cited in this context which demonstrate the favour Madeira wine enjoyed among the British. Shakespeare (1564-1616) had Falstaff say in "Henry the IV": "that Malmsey-nosed knave Bardolph." About Falstaff, Shakespeare wrote further that he sold his soul for a glass of Madeira and a leg of capon. Duke George of Clarency was sentenced to death in 1478. As a nobleman, he was permitted to choose the method of execution; he chose to drown in a vat of Malvasier! Since then, one type of Madeira has borne his name. In London today, honorary citizens are toasted with a glass of Madeira.

Even the Americans have always highly prized Madeira wine. They celebrated the signing of the Declaration of Independence with a glass of Madeira.

The wine trade flourished, and was interrupted only during the 60 years of Spanish rule (1580-1640).

it was more a coincidence that Madeira wine took on its present composition. On one journey to the British Indian colonies, the wine could not be delivered to the customer and had to be shipped back to Madeira. There it was discovered that the taste had improved considerably. After some experiments, the conclusion was reached that the improved taste could be attributed to crossing the equator twice. As a result, all subsequent wines underwent this refinement, being shipped back and forth across the equator. Later it was noted that not the equator but rather the warm temperatures and increased aging were responsible for the wine's transformation. Thanks to the development of artificial warming techniques, this difficult method of making "vinho da roda" ("wine of the circle," so called because of "rounding the globe") was abandoned at the end of the 18th century.

Madeira also owes its present quality in part to Napoleon. The sea blockade ordered by the French emperor also affected the Portuguese kingdom as allies of England. The decline in trade caused an excess of brandy and Madeira to accumulate on the island. To increase the longevity of the wine, brandy was added to it. This "spiked" wine had an even better flavour, and thereafter, brandy was always added to the casks.

In the 19th century, Madeira wineries suffered a great blow which almost led to their complete demise. Between 1851 and 1856, the mildew Oidium tuckeri destroyed nearly all of the grapevines. Only the application of sulphur saved a few of them. On top of that came the grape-louse plague (Phyloxera vastatrix) in 1873, which almost put an end to Madeira wine. Only by planting American grapevines, whose roots are resistant to grape lice, could the remaining Madeira grapes be saved. In the critical mildew and plague period, the supplies of Madeira were almost completely exhausted, so that during the years of regeneration, nothing of the right age and high quality was left as a basis for the Solera wines. To support the wine trade and insure the livelihood of many farmers and vintners, wine productions codes were modified to allow the making of lesser quality wines. Since January 1, 1980, the state-run *Instituto da Vinha e do Vinho da Madeira* (winery and wine institute), or IVM for short, has been in charge of quality control and wine production, and is also involved in advertising for the wines.

The main importers are traditionally Great Britain and the US, but Japan, Switzerland, Austria, and the EC nations are also good customers.

Portugal's membership in the EC has, of course, also had consequences for Madeira's wine growers. The EC subsidises farmers who grow high-quality grapes. The switch to high-quality grapes is not without problems for the farmers, since the vines need seven years before bearing fruit.

Wine / **Production**

The sweet varieties grow at lower elevations, the dry Sercial thrives even at 800 metres (2,616 feet), and Verdelho grows well at elevations of up to 500 metres (1,600 feet). The higher up the vines are planted, the lower the sugar content and thus the drier the taste. The main growing regions are Estreito de Câmara de Lobos, Câmara de Lobos, Ponta do Pargo, and Campanário. Machinery cannot be used on Madeira's terraced fields; thus, everything is done by hand in growing Madeira wine. The grapevines grow on racks or frames, under which vegetables are usually planted; every inch of land on this mountainous island is used! The vines need about seven years after planting before yielding harvestable grapes: On Madeira there are about 4,500 vineyards, none of which produces more than seven barrels a year. Thus, high-quality Madeira is always in short supply! The plants bloom in April. Grapes are harvested in August and September; they are picked by hand. They are brought to central collection points in baskets, and from there driven to the wine presses. Farmers are paid according to the weight of the grapes. Earlier, they pressed the must themselves in the remote and inaccessible regions; the must was then brought in *borrachos* to the vintners. *Borrachos* are tanned goat-skins used as vessels. In the past, grapes were stomped by foot; today, this is usually accomplished with machines. To ferment, the must is put into bottles, and wine distillate is added to the good varieties. The days are gone when brandy was used. At this stage, the IVM has an influence since it imports the alcohol for all vintners on Madeira. After fermentation and fortification, the must is kept at 35 to 50 °C (95 to 122 °F) for at least 3 months *(estufagem)*. There are three estufagen methods: the least expensive and most common method is to heat the wine in huge tanks (up to 50,000 litres/13,000 gallons). In the second method, wooden barrels are stored in a house kept at 45 °C (113 °F). The "estufas do sol" allows the vats to be warmed only by the sun — this is the most expensive, time-consuming method and is hardly used anymore. Good quality wines are kept warm for 6 to 12 months; heating, storage, and evaporation are expensive processes for the vintner. The alcohol distillate is added to the less expensive varieties after they have cooled. The wine is then filled into barrels to age. The longer the aging process lasts, the higher the quality of wine. Employees of the IVM seal the barrels at the beginning of this stage, and samples may be taken only in the presence of a member of the IVM. Thus, dilution attempts are prevented. Quality wines are only those which have aged in the barrel for 15 to 20 years and in the bottle for at least another 2 years. The minimum time needed for maturation is one year, and a good wine is at least 3 years old before being bottled. The IVM checks the chemical composition of the wine and its taste. A commission of 6 judges (3 from IVM, 3 from alternating wineries) tests the wine for quality. Only then does the wine receive its seal of approval which must appear on each bottle.

Wines / **Tours and Tasting**

The largest wineries are all located in Funchal. Most offer guided tours. All wine producers ship abroad.

Madeira Wine Company: Avenida Arriaga 28, Tel: 2 01 21, open Monday to Friday from 9 am to 7 pm; Saturday, from 9 am to 1 pm. Tours Monday to Friday at 10:30 am and 3 pm, 400$00.

The Madeira Wine Company was founded in 1913 by several shippers. Today, the MWC is a group of different wineries who coordinate their production and sales, yet each winery maintains its self-sufficiency and of course the characteristics of its own wine. Some of the best-known brands are Blandys, Cossarts, Leacocks, Miles, Welsh Brothers, and Luis Gomes. A wine and souvenir shop with numerous books on wine is a sign of well-organized marketing. The tours are extensive and given in English and French. Included in the tour are the company's own wine museum with old equipment, presses, and borrachos, viewing a film, and wine tasting.

One of Funchal's oldest streets belongs to the MWC, as does the São Francisco chapel found on it.

Pereira d'Oliveira: Rua dos Ferreiros 107, Tel: 2 07 84; open Monday to Friday from 9 am to 12:30 pm and 2:30 to 6 pm; Saturday, from 9:30 am to 12:30 pm. This is a Madeiran family business with a long tradition. On Rua dos Ferreiros is also a sales and exhibition room. Upon request, wine making is explained in English or French, and one can taste the wine.

Casa dos Vinhos da Madeira: Rua do Netos 40 and Rua dos Ferreiros 125 (two entrances), Tel: 3 67 67; open Monday to Friday from 10 am to 1:30 pm and 3 to 6 pm; Saturday, from 10 am to 1 pm. Casados vinhos belongs to the Henriques & Henriques company, formerly a family business with a long tradition, which owns vineyards near Estreito de Câmara de Lobos and Câmara de Lobos. After the last Henrique died without an heir at the age of 90 in 1968, the winery was taken over by several shareholders, also reputable vintners. There is a "Taste and Buy" bar for the Henriques & Henriques wines.

Vinhos Barbeito: Estrada Monumental 145, Tel: 2 94 34/2 33 29. The cellars invite tourists, and one is given a more authentic look at wine production. At the back is a small tasting room, in which one can admire (or buy) the firm's treasures — for instance, a Madeira from 1795 for 75,000$00. The tours are improvised; therefore, not very professional, and actually only in Portuguese or broken English. "Diogos Wine Shop" on Avenida Arriaga 48, open Monday to Friday from 9 am to 12:30 pm and 2 to 7 pm, is Vinhos Barbeito's wine shop and is more geared to tourists and visitors. An interesting fact: Manuela Barbeito is the only female vintner in the otherwise male-dominated world of Madeiran wine.

Artur de Barros e Sousa: Rua dos Ferreiros 109, Tel: 2 06 22, open Monday to Friday from 9 am to 12:30 pm and 2:30 to 5:30 pm. This small, family business, which was almost lost among the sales rooms of "Casa do Vinho" and "Pereira d'Oliveira" targeting mainly tourists is the only winery on Madeira that still produces superb quality "vinho de canteiro." Here, one can also taste and buy the family's wine, and especially interested parties are shown the cellars upon request.

A truly family-oriented and traditional atmosphere is felt when Senhor de Barros lovingly tells about his wine (only in Portuguese or French).

Museu do Instituto do Vinho da Madeira: Rua 5 de Outobro 78, open from 9:30 am to noon and 2 to 5 pm; admission is free of charge.

The museum at the wine institute exhibits old wine presses, cork and label machines, borrachos, and old photos and sketches by Max Römer. This German painter lived on Madeira with his family from 1922 to 1960 and depicted life on the island very accurately and in great detail.